Contents

Introduction	Page 2
Facts & Figures about Lanzarote	Page 3
Healthcare	Page 15
Banking	Page 21
Paperwork	Page 23
Property	Page 30
Pets	Page 35
Cars	Page 41
Utilities	Page 57
What to do in an emergency	Page 61
Schooling & kids	Page 69
Shopping	Page 93
Telephones, mobiles and internet	Page 108
Business and Jobs	Page 119
The End!	Page 133

Introduction

Welcome to this Camel Guide to relocating to Lanzarote. I guess you're reading it because you're planning or hoping to move the this lovely island one day.

There are many benefits to living here, and we haven't looked back since we made the move ourselves at the turn of the century.

The contents here are an aggregation of four year's work. We've selected the relevant parts from the 5,000 or so articles we've written and published on Lanzarote Information over the years, and put them in one place so you can easily access them.

We've deliberately left the links in the various articles – if you are reading this on a computer or tablet, you will be able to click them and view additional content on our website. If you're on a E Reader, you probably won't.

Things change fast in Spain, particularly in relation to paperwork! We'll always do our best to keep this guide up to date, but if you do find something that isn't correct, please let us know by emailing jules@lanzaroteinformation.com

We hope you find this guide helpful in your planning, and we look forward to running into sometime here in Lanzarote!

Facts and Figures About Lanzarote

Population and land

These figures are based on a Cabildo report. Like most government reports, it's lengthy, boring and overly complicated, and of course, it's in Spanish! However, on your behalf, we have waded through it for you, and we have uncovered some amazing and interesting facts. Perfect information if you know and love Lanzarote, and brilliant snippets for you to quote while you're out and about with friends having a drink or a bite!

Lanzarote is the fourth largest of the Canary Islands, it is divided up into 7 municipalities - Arrecife (the capital), Haría, San Bartolomé, Teguise, Tías, Tinajo, and Yaiza. The island of La Graciosa is included in the area of Teguise.

The island covers 850 square kilometres, and each municipality comes out like this:
Arrecife 22.7 km2
Haría 106.6 km2
San Bartolomé 40.9 km2
Teguise 264 km2
Tías 64.6 km2
Tinajo 135.3 km2
Yaiza 211.8 km2

Arrecife is just 20M above sea level and the Castillo at Teguise is at 305 metres height.. The castle was built as a protection from pirates, so it's no accident that it's at

the top of the island.
Almost half the island's land mass (42%) is protected, and these areas include Timanfaya and La Graciosa.

The population of the island has almost doubled in 10 years, in 1996 the figure was 77,379 and in 2007 this had increased to 132,366. This is spread over the following municipalities:

Arrecife 56,834
Haría 5,049
San Bartolomé 18,050
Teguise 17,688
Tías 18,263
Tinajo 5,588
Yaiza 10,894

In terms of population density therefore, Arrecife is obviously the densest with 2,500 residents per square kilometre and Tinajo the least with just 41.

The population in Lanzarote is a fairly even split between men who number 68,845 and women who total 63,521, the highest population is grouped in the ages from 25 to 44 years old, so we're a young island, especially compared to most European countries.

The town with the least population was La Geria with 23 residents, which emphasises how these figures can be skewed as there are obviously many more people living in the town, but many have holiday homes there and live in other parts of the island where they are registered.

The population of La Graciosa is 640, although this swells daily with visitors who come over on the ferry from Orzola.

The resident population in the resorts is as follows:

Costa Teguise 5,713
Playa Blanca 7,956
Puerto del Carmen 10,315

Lanzarote is a transient island and we have lots of different nationalities living here, please note these population figures are based on registered residents and the actual figures are much higher! Many of the people living here from other countries are not registered as residents and live and work "off the books".

Of the figure of 132,366, there are 98,725 Spanish residents, 3,549 German, 1,530 Italians, 5,909 British, 3,205 Morrocans and 5,175 Columbians. The perceived wisdom is that there are probably double that number of Brits living here. We also have a large number of Chinese and Indian residents on the Lanzarote, running restaurants and camera shops, but I was surprised at the official figures which show Chinese and Indian at just 859 and 640 respectively.

Economy

The Cabildo categorizes businesses on the island in the following sectors and the changes over the last eight years are interesting:

No of Companies From 1999 - To 2007

Industrial 367 - 508
Construction 754 - 1,754
Comercial 3,001 - 3,829
Hotels 1,493 - 2,042
Transport 712 - 889
Other Services 2,212 - 4,504

Total 8,539 - 13,526

So in percentage terms the biggest growth has come in the construction sector, and overall the number of registered businesses on the island has increased by 55% in the last eight years.

During 2007 a total of just over 3,000 new building projects were granted permission, with almost 80% of them being for dwellings, as opposed to tourist accommodation.

Delving deeper, we find that estate agents grew in number in the same period from 268 to 1,099! Cultivated land on the island grew from 3,094 hectares to 4,435, with just over 3,000 dedicated to wine production, 60% of which is growing the Malvasia grape variety. Back in 1999, there were just four registered wine bodegas here, and now there are 20. The years

1999 and 2001 were designated "top quality" for Lanzarote made wine.

Staying with farming, we learn that the number of goats on the island has doubled during this period to more than 25,000, and that there are 341 camels on the island, all bar two living in Yaiza. The odd pair live in Haria - perhaps they are retired?

Fishing remains an important industry for the island and there are 129 ship builders and repairers in Lanzarote, looking after 143 registered fishing boats, crewed by 349 licensed fishermen.

In terms of work contracts, there are just over 60,000 registered workers on the island, split 33,000 men and 27,000 women. In 2007, there were around 7,000 on the dole, up from the all time low in 2000 of just 2,358 people.

Tourism Facts

In our final part of the facts and figures series, we're going to look at three areas:

The Weather
Tourism
Vehicles

The Weather

This is the question I'm most often asked about the island: "What's the weather like?" And the truth is that those of us who live here don't really take much notice of the weather, and we for sure don't watch TV forecasts, which are always wrong!

Here are the facts about the weather in Lanzarote for 2007. Rain was recorded on 44 days, but there was none at all in June, July, August and September. In fact from March until November there were less than 100MM of rainfall for the eight months. This is about the same level of rain you can expect in Manchester in a typical December! We did have two months of quite heavy rain - both January and December recorded more than 300MM.

The average maximum temperature throughout 2007 was 29.6 degrees, with a high of 42 degrees in July, but May, August, October and November all attained more than 30 degrees on at least one day. The coldest we measured was 11.5 degrees during March, and the average low was 15.3 degrees. From July to October, the temperature did not fall below 18 degrees at any time of day.

Tourism

Tourism is the life blood of the island, and contributes either directly or indirectly to all our livelihoods on this small island.

Overall we had 1.6 million tourists visiting the island in 2007. Those from the United Kingdom were far and away the largest group, with more than 800,000, followed by Germany with 313,000 and Ireland with 210,000. One fascinating statistic is that the airport recorded more than 5 Million arrivals in the year, which shows how many flights were taken to and from other countries by residents and how many people flew in to stay in their own properties, or in privately rented villas, as the above figures are for holidays booked with tour operators.

The airports feeding the largest number of passengers in to Lanzarote are Madrid and Gran Canaria, and the UK airport sending the most traffic to the island is Manchester, followed by London Gatwick. The top three airlines with flights from UK were First Choice, Thomson Fly and Thomas Cook, in that order.
Overall, tourists visiting the island dropped a fraction (0.01%), but there were some significant rises and falls when broken down by country. UK tourism dropped 5%, Germany 7% and France a whopping 34%. But rises were recorded from the Spanish mainland (7%) and Ireland (6%).

THIS FACT IS WORTHY OF CAPITALS. MORE THAN 423,000 IRISH PEOPLE VISITED LANZAROTE IN 2007. CONSIDERING THEIR POPULATION IS 4.2 MILLION PEOPLE, THAN MEANS 1 IN 10 PEOPLE FROM IRELAND VISITED LANZAROTE IN 2007!

In the part of Arrecife we had a quarter of a million further visitors on cruise ships and ferries. Cruising has been the biggest growth area in the island by miles. As recently as 1991 just 31,000 cruise tourists came to the island, and last year the number rose to more than 216,000.

One and a half million tonnes of goods were imported through Puerto Naos, and just 178,000 were exported. Close to a million people travelled on the ferries from Playa Blanca to Fuerteventura and 2007 saw a huge rise in the number of people visiting La Graciosa via the Orzola ferry - almost 250,000 people made the trip compared to 16,000 in 1998. This reinforces the belief that tourists are now travelling and exploring much more of the island than previously.

Vehicles

At the end of 2007, there were 120,000 vehicles and nearly 4,000 motorcycles registered for the road, almost one per person of population - this has doubled since 1996.

There are 407 taxis on the island, with half registered in Arrecife and Tias. Taxis can only collect fares from their own area, which is why even an empty Arrecife taxi will not answer a hail in Puerto del Carmen, for example.

Nearly 12,000 new cars were registered in 2007, with a third being in the Tias area. Just 57 were registered in Haria.

There were 235 road accidents in 2007, with a total of ten fatalities. Considering the on going debate about driving standards on the island, those figures seem low to me.

Choosing where to live in Lanzarote

The chances are you've holidayed a few times on the island, and the obvious choice is to choose to live in the area you know. But don't forget being on holiday is very different to living here.

Broadly speaking, I'd break down the island's areas as follows:

The resorts – **Puerto del Carmen, Costa Teguise** and **Playa Blanca**

The towns – Places like **Arrecife**, **Teguise**, **Playa Honda**, San Bartolome, Tias and Yaiza

Rural areas – Places like La Asomada, **Haria, Arrieta, Femes** and pretty much anywhere north of Teguise

Each has advantages and disadvantages:

The Resorts

There are many benefits to living in a resort area. You are more likely to find work, the shops are open long hours and are well stocked, and many people speak English. You'll also find many other ex pats live in resort areas, so it may be much easier to create a network of friends. Internet connection for home or by using **wi-fi hotspots** is also pretty straightforward.

The downsides of living in a resort include the fact that shopping for food in the local supermarkets can be expensive, your Spanish may not improve, and you may be subjected to noisy holidaymakers! Prices of property, for rental or purchase tend to be higher and the properties themselves are often smaller.

The Towns

The island's towns are home to the bulk of the population, and are a good place to set up home. You'll find fewer "English" goods in the shops, but they will offer better value. **Internet connection** is no problem and you'll be able to get a high speed service in the towns – there's even cable now in Arrecife. You'll find property prices are lower and the houses and apartments much more spacious.

You'll also find you are more easily able to make local contacts, as your neighbours will also be living here, rather than on holiday.

You might struggle with outdoor space, though, and unless you're in Arrecife, you won't be near the beach and are unlikely to have access to a swimming pool. Apart from fiesta time, the towns are generally quieter than the resorts.

Rural Areas

You'll have the chance to really "feel" Spanish by living in a rural area. You may still see people working the land with donkeys, you'll be dealing a lot with small shopkeepers, and you'll enjoy much more space, both inside and outside properties. Many villages still revolve around their Sociedads, and you'll find you soon become a part of village life if you frequent yours.

Rentals and house prices are generally the lowest in rural areas.

Most village shops still observe siesta, and you won't find English style food or newspapers in them. They are, however, great value for money and offer old fashioned, courteous service. The internet has reached most parts of the island now, although speeds in rural areas can be as low as 1MB, and there are still parts of the island where **mobile phone** signals are weak. Very few people in rural areas speak any English

Get a copy of the story of one family's move to Lanzarote: **Living in Lanzarote**

Health Care

State Health Service in Lanzarote

The health service and healthcare in Lanzarote is excellent. Whilst there is a thriving private medical care system here, we'll focus on the state provided version in this article and cover the private sector in a follow up.

To access the national health service here, you need a social security card or to have a travel form from your country within the European Union.

The health system works on three levels: First, there are the Farmacias (Pharmacies), then we have the Centros de Salud (Doctor's surgeries) and finally the Hospital General (General Hospital).

The pharmacies here are much more empowered than in many other Eurpoean countries - pharmacists can sell drugs which are often on prescription elsewhere. For that reason, most people with minor ailments will visit a pharmacy and buy what is required over the counter, following advice from the pharmacist.

There are doctor's surgeries in most towns and villages and you should register at your local one. As well as providing help and prescriptions when you are ill, they also have comprehensive preventatitve program and will ask you in at least once a year for a series of tests. For example you will be regularly tested for diabetes as the disease is prevalent in The Canary Islands for some reason and nobody knows why.

The top tier in the health service is the Hospital General José Molina in Arrecife. This is a top notch hospital with good facilities, as well as a full accident and emergency centre. Many of the staff speak English, and visiting times are pretty relaxed. Wards are divided into rooms with only two patients per room with a shared en suite bathroom. Televisions are provided and there are plenty of staff, as well as decent meals. For visitors, there's a terrific Cafeteria which provides freshly made, great value food at all hours and the best coffee in Arrecife!

Nobody wants you to be ill in Lanzarote, but if you are, you can rest assured that you will be well looked after.

General Hospital

The main general and emergency hospital in Arrecife is called Hospital Doctor José Molina Orosa, it is situated on the road leaving Arrecife up the hill to San Bartolomé, when you exit the circunvalacion, pull into the left hand lane past the petrol station and at the roundabout take your first exit, the car park is on the right as you enter the hospital grounds and there is a taxi rank outside. The visiting hours are officially from 13:00 to 21:00, they don't tend to be too strict about it but you may be stopped from accessing the wards outside these times.

Reception is found through the first green sliding door on the front of the building, the second door is for patients and the door on the front left hand corner is the waiting room for families. The hospital will only allow one visitor to the patient whilst being treated in the emergency wards, it is common for the whole family to wait in reception for news, it can be cold and there are toilets and a water machine. Refreshments are available from the cafeteria opposite the main entrance to the hospital.

Hospital Doctor José Molina Orosa
Carretera San Bartolomé KM 1'300
35500 Arrecife (Lanzarote)
Telephone: (0034) 928 595 000

Doctor's appointments

Once you have registered with your local doctor, to make an appointment it's best to call the central service on 012, they will take your name and telephone contact details and give you a time to visit the local surgery. If you prefer you can make an appointment online **Cita Previa** you need to enter your CIP code from your medical card.

Please note, if you need urgent medical attention, call 112.

If you are not a pensioner with entitlement to medical care or paying seguridad social you will not receive local medical care at a centro salud, you will need to pay for a private clinic / hospital or use your **European Health Card** for an emergency visit to the hospital.

Vaccinations for children

Concerned parents have contacted us for advice about vaccinations offered to children in the Canary Islands, with particular reference to babies under two years old when they are relocating to live in the islands.

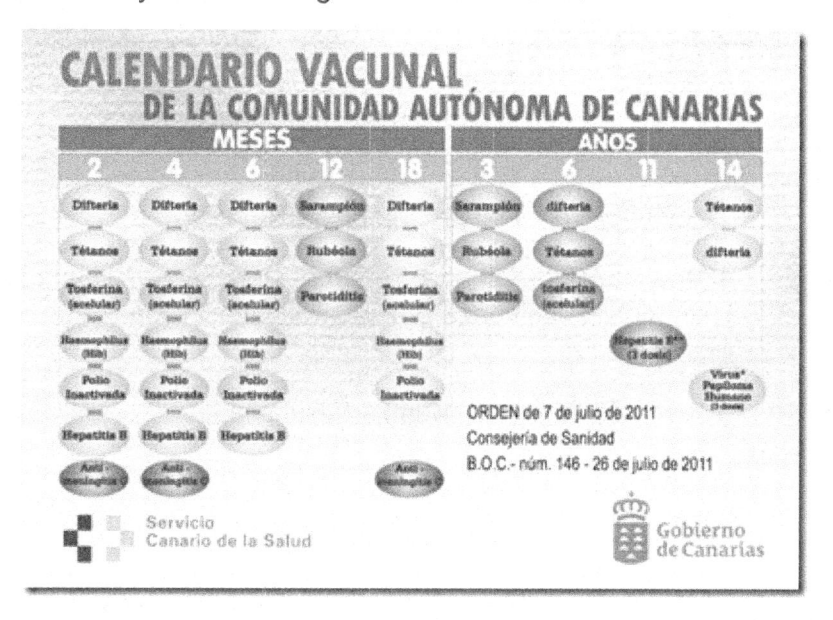

CALENDARIO VACUNAL
DE LA COMUNIDAD AUTÓNOMA DE CANARIAS

MESES					AÑOS			
2	4	6	12	18	3	6	11	14
Difteria	Difteria	Difteria	Sarampión	Difteria	Sarampión	difteria		Tétanos
Tétanos	Tétanos	Tétanos	Rubéola	Tétanos	Rubéola	Tétanos		difteria
Tosferina (acelular)	Tosferina (acelular)	Tosferina (acelular)	Parotiditis	Tosferina (acelular)	Parotiditis	tosferina (acelular)		
Haemophilus (Hib)	Haemophilus (Hib)	Haemophilus (Hib)		Haemophilus (Hib)			Hepatitis B** (3 dosis)	
Polio Inactivada	Polio Inactivada	Polio Inactivada		Polio Inactivada				Virus* Papiloma Humano (3 dosis)
Hepatitis B	Hepatitis B	Hepatitis B						
Anti meningitis C	Anti meningitis C			Anti meningitis C				

ORDEN de 7 de julio de 2011
Consejería de Sanidad
B.O.C.- núm. 146 - 26 de julio de 2011

Servicio Canario de la Salud

Gobierno de Canarias

The above chart shows the various vaccinations offered to children from 2 months through to 14 years old in relation to the Canary Islands. The Calendario Vacunal for the Canary Islands was last updated in July 2011.

Children registered with the local health service (Servico Canario de la Salud) will be vaccinated at the following ages:

2 months old: Diptheria, Tetanus, Tosferina (acelular), Haemophilus Influenza B (Hib), Polio Inactivada, Hepatitis B & Anti Meningitis C

4 months old: Diptheria, Tetanus, Tosferina (acelular), Haemophilus Influenza B (Hib), Polio Inactivada, Hepatitis B & Anti Meningitis C

6 months old: Diptheria, Tetanus, Tosferina (acelular), Haemophilus Influenza B (Hib), Polio Inactivada & Hepatitis B

12 months old: Measels, Mumps & Rubella

18 months old: Diptheria, Tetanus, Tosferina (acelular), Haemophilus Influenza B (Hib), Polio Inactivada & Anti Meningitis C

3 years old: Measels, Mumps & Rubella

6 years old: Diptheria, Tetanus & Tosferina (acelular)

11 years old: Hepatitis B (3 doses)

14 yeard old: Tetanus, Diptheria & Human PapillomaVirus (HPV) (3 doses)

At the last update, the triple MMR vaccine was changed to be administered at 12 months old instead of 15 due to an increase in outbreaks within the country.

Banking

It is easy to open a bank account in Lanzarote, until recently you only needed to walk into any branch with your passport and ask for a resident or non-resident account. Now you will be asked for a copy of your NIE/F number which is your Número de Identidad de Extranjeros / Número de Identificación Fiscal. If you don't have one of these it will be necessary to visit the new police station in Arrecife and one will be issued to you within 3 days with the current process.

There is a wide range of banks available on the island, including Barclays located in Arrecife, but don't get too excited, they are part of Barclays but you can't action anything from your UK accounts at this branch and to my knowledge they don't have any counter staff speaking English.

Solbank are aimed at the expat community, they have a branch in each resort and all of their staff speak a minimum of 3 languages Spanish, German and English. Their branches are modern, air conditioned and there is always a personal welcome and no waiting in long queues for the counter service. They have a very good online service available in English and can offer excellent sterling saving accounts. www.solbank.com

La Caixa are typically a Spanish bank but with a very high expat following, they have a branch in each resort but also in municipality towns such as Tías, San Bartolomé and of course Arrecife. Most of their counter staff can speak English and you can change the language on their online banking system. Because of their popularity, you will find that often you are queueing for counter services, its a social event, I don't think I can walk into the local branch and not bump into someone I know there. **www.lacaixa.es**

There are other banks but in my opinion if you're looking for good personal service, easy accessible locations and English speaking staff either of these banks are the best.

Paperwork

How to register with the town hall (ayuntamiento).

This document is very useful and only available to residents with Spanish residencia.

Essentially it registers you on the electoral roll with your local town hall, you need your passport, residencia and proof of address so either a rent contract or escritura. The first time you register on the island you need to allow 14 days for the process, if you move areas or want a replacement at a later date they are either issued immediately or within 3 days. Some ayuntamiento's will ask for a small fee and others provide this document free. It is possible that the police will call at your address to check that you actually live there during the process, they do check occasionally!

When you have registered you then need to request the certificate, this can only be requested and collected in person as proof of ID is required.

You will be asked a reason why you want the certificate, it could be for a school place, to buy a car, for cheap travel within Spain, residents rate water etc.

NIF and NIE Numbers

The local system here changes frequently, at the time of this update you can apply for a N.I.E. number and receive the documents within a few working days.

If you are moving to Lanzarote to live here for more than six months then apply for your residencia not the N.I.E number as you will receive this at the same time.

If you are buying a property in Lanzarote but will remain a non-resident then you will need to apply for your N.I.E number.

N.I.E Number

The N.I.E. is short for Número de Identidad / Identificación de Extranjero this identifies you as a foreigner.

N.I.F. Number

The N.I.F. is short for Número de Identificación Fiscal, this is your tax identification.

If you are asked for your D.N.I. you can either provide your residencia certificate or N.I.E. document.

Why do you need one of these numbers?

Basically it is an identification that the Spanish Authorities can verify who you are. It proves that you are in Spain legally and proof of this will normally be asked when you:

Buy a car / property
Start work
Open a bank account
Order services such as telephone or electric

What do I need to apply for the N.I.E.?

When you have a local address, complete **form EX14**, take a photocopy of this form, two residencia sized photographs (30mm x 25mm) together with your valid passport and a photocopy to the:

COMISARÍA DE POLICÍA

C/ Mastelero, s/n, 35500, Arrecife, Lanzarote, Las Palmas

Telephone: 928 844 266

Opening hours: Monday to Friday from 9am to 2pm

There is a small charge (under €10) payable to a designated bank account, details of which will be confirmed at the police station.

When submitted, the photocopy of the form will be given to you with an appointment to return and collect your N.I.E.

How does this become my N.I.F.?

If you have bought a property it is important to make sure that your N.I.E. number has been registered with the Spanish inland revenue which is called AEAT so that it is also your N.I.F. number.

Residencia

There is some paperwork to complete when you relocate to live in on a permanent basis in Lanzarote. My advice would be to tackle one thing at a time, expect some difficulties and consider employing a paperwork expert to help you if you get stuck.

Currently extranjeros (foreigners) are only provided with a sheet of A4 green paper which is your certificate to show you are resident in Spain. You should notify the Oficina de Extranjeros if you are planning to stay longer than three months, although your main residence is still determined by the country you live in for more than 6 months of the year.

For residencia you need to visit the Oficina de Extranjeros which is located in the Comisaría de Policía building in the Puerto Naos area of Arrecife.

COMISARÍA DE POLICÍA

C/ Mastelero, s/n, 35500, Arrecife, Lanzarote, Las Palmas

Telephone: 928 844 266

Opening hours: Monday to Friday from 9am to 2pm

To apply for residencia you need to complete the form EX18, supply three residencia sized photographs (30mm x 25mm) and show a valid passport and your rent contract, escritura (property deeds) or certificado de empadronamiento as proof of residence in Spain.

There is now an English & German speaking representative at the police station who can help with the application if you don't speak Spanish.

When you arrive, approach the man at the desk on the right hand side, explain that you would like to become resident in Lanzarote and he will give you a copy of the form EX-18 and Modelo 790 together with an appointment to come back. I have attached copies of these forms below just for your information.

There is a fee of €10.20, this is paid at any bank using the TASA Modelo 790 form you were given. Next complete the form EX-18 solicitud de certificado de registro de residencia comunitaria where indicated and take the originals plus copies of all your documents back with you to the police station.

You will need to allow for at least two visits to the police station during the process, one to collect the forms, the next to submit the forms, the third to collect your residencia certificate. The good news is that the process is short and it is possible to obtain your residencia within a week.

As the current form of the residencia does not have a photo identification this document is not classed as ID and must be supported with a valid passport. The residencia certificate is valid for 10 years if it states "residente comunitario con caracter permanente en Espana" otherwise it is valid for 5 years

Property

Buying a property

If you are considering purchasing property in Lanzarote, we think you should consider the following questions:

Why?
Is the property for you to use, is it purely an investment property to holiday or long term rent or are you buying it to live here?

Where?
If you are buying an investment property to rent you should consider the tourist areas, for maximum rental potential. If you are buying for your own use, do you want a holiday property or something more residential? Have you considered rural areas for example?

When?
Are you looking to purchase now, maybe buy something off plan, or looking for some time in the future?

How?
Do you have the funds available to buy outright or are you going to require a mortgage or are you waiting to sell another property? You will need a minimum deposit of 30-40% of the purchase price to cover the deposit and costs, a non resident mortgage is usually up to 70% of the sales price / valuation and a resident 80%.

Choosing the property
Once you have viewed a selection of properties and narrowed it down to a shortlist of 1 or 2 then you need to

take a closer look at the area, community, noise level etc. It may be wise to revisit the property at a different time of day if you are unsure of the location. There are strict building regulations on the island and if you are planning to extend or add a swimming pool it would be advisable to check with the local Ayuntamiento that the necessary licences will be authorised.

Reserving a property

Unlike the UK it is normal to pay a deposit of 10% of the purchase price to reserve a property. Normally you will pay an initial deposit to reserve a property and the balance of the 10% within 14 days.

NIF

You cannot purchase a property without an **NIE/F number**. Once you have decided on a property to purchase and have reserved it, you will need to visit the police station in Arrecife for a NIE/F number. If you are moving to the island, you should apply for residencia as you will be offered up to 80% mortgage terms and capital gains tax advantages. If you are not sure about the residencia, please take financial advice in the UK as to your personal circumstances.

Bank Account & Mortgage

You will need a bank account to own a property in Lanzarote, they are easy to open and just require your passport and NIE/F number.

If you require a mortgage on the property you need to decide which bank is the right one for you, some of them are better at languages, or have more branches, better interest rates or no fees to pay off lump sums. A resident can have up to 80% of the sales price and a non-resident can have up to 70%. Most banks offer quotations and approval subject to valuation in around 24 hours unless more information is required. Once the bank has approved your mortgage, they will request a valuation report, which compares your property to similar ones in the surrounding area, this gives the bank an indication of the value and condition of the property. You pay for this as part of your purchase costs but will be given a copy for your information too.

Lawyer

Although you can purchase a property without a lawyer, we strongly recommend that you do use one to check that the property has legal title and is free of debt. Normally within 2 weeks, your lawyer or agent will draw up a purchase contract for both parties to sign. This contract confirms the buyer and seller, the price agreed, the deposit paid, the property details, a completion date and provides protection to either side if one defaults. The standard term is that if the vendor defaults they have to refund double the amount of deposit paid and if the purchaser defaults they lose their deposit paid. Once this contact has been signed and exchanged, the 10% deposit is paid to the vendor pending the completion of the notary. This is a great system and although not 100% guaranteed, there are few sales that don't complete after this point.

Foreign Currency Transfers

If you are transferring a considerable amount of money from the UK for your purchase we would advise you to watch the **exchange rates** and transfer accordingly to reach an optimum price for your sterling. There are now many reputable international currency brokers that you can set an agreement with to transfer funds at a predetermined rate or alternatively your own bank in the UK can arrange an international money transfer.

On average a sale is completed in 4-6 weeks unless otherwise specified. Normally the NIE/F number, bank account and lawyer will be completed whilst you are still in Lanzarote, you may need to send information from the UK for your mortgage application such as proof of income and a credit report/rating. Once the mortgage has been approved and the valuation report received, the notary can be booked to sign after 5 working days. At this point you should have transferred the balance funds so that they will have cleared on your local account in time for the signing.

Notary day
Whilst you may be nervous at the thought of attending a Notary, these can quite often be a long wait and a bit of an anti climax! It's normally an early start on the day and your estate agent may accompany you as well as your lawyer to the designated notary. You normally need to go to the bank first to sign the mortgage papers and authorise the payments for the notary. From the bank you head to the notary where you have to provide your identification which is your passport and NIE/F or residencia, the notary will then prepare your escritura for the property and mortgage if required. Once the paperwork is ready you will be taken by an official translator to have the escritura and mortgage details read to you in English - this is your opportunity to ask any questions. Once you have checked and agreed these documents you are normally waiting for the bank

manager to arrive with the money! You can be waiting a few hours in the Notary, we would advise you to take a drink and food if you think you will need it and something to keep any accompanying children amused. The actual procedure in front of the Notary takes approximately 15 minutes where they read the escritura aloud in Spanish and both parties sign the documents including your translator. You will need to pay the translator at the Notary so make sure that you have extra cash towards your costs with you. Although the keys are normally exchanged on this day you don't actually own the property until the sale is registered and the taxes paid.

What happens next?
A week after the Notary your escritura will be available to collect from the Notary which your bank or your lawyer will do along with paying the purchase tax of 6.5% to the Registro de la Propiedad in Arrecife. Your laywer will contact the services and community to transfer the water, electric and community charges to your details.

Pets

Bringing a pet to the island

A pet's passport is recommended for any cats or dogs that are travelling abroad with you. This ensures that they can return to the UK once 6 months has passed and they have a valid rabies vaccination.

Details of the Pet Travel Scheme can be found on the **Defra website**.

Allow at least 6 weeks before your departure date to start this process with your vet. Your animal will have to be chipped and vaccinated and complete a health check before being allowed to travel.

We strongly recommend that you shop around when looking for a carrier for your pet and try to book a daytime flight. It is possible to book your pets on most airlines so that they can travel in the cargo section at the same time as you.

When you arrive at the **Arrecife Airport** and have collected your suitcases, you will need to make your way to the separate cargo building where a guardia civil officer will check your pets papers and that they are not on the local **dangerous animals** list. Payment for the flight and kennel has to be paid in advance and the local clearing agent will charge on arrival for customs and clearing if your UK agent has not prearranged this.

The travel kennel will be released with the animal, you can leave this at customs if it is not required or there is a charity organisation on the island (**SARA**) who will be grateful for the box if you can fit it in your car!

Dangerous Dogs

According to the Ley 50/1999 passed by Royal Decree in March 2002, the following list of dog breeds are considered to be dangerous in Spain including any cross breeds:

a) Pit Bull Terrier

b) Staffordshire Bull Terrier

c) American Staffordshire Terrier

d) Rottweiler

e) Dogo Argentino

f) Fila Brasileiro

g) Tosa Inu

h) Akita Inu

In addition the law states that dogs included in Ley 50/1999 have a majority of the following characteristics:

a) Fuerte musculatura, aspecto poderoso, robusto, configuración atlética, agilidad, vigor y resistencia (strong muscles, powerful, robust aspect, athletic configuration, agility, vigor and resistance)

b) Marcado carácter y gran valor (noticeable character and great value)

c) Pelo corto (short hair)

d) Perímetro torácico comprendido entre 60 y 80 centímetros, altura a la cruz entre 50 y 70 centímetros y peso superior a 20 kg (thorasic perimiter between 60 and 80 cm, height to the cross between 50 and 70 cm and weight heavier than 20 kg)

e) Cabeza voluminosa, cuboide, robusta, con cráneo ancho y grande y mejillas musculosas y abombadas. Mandíbulas grandes y fuertes, boca robusta, ancha y profunda. (Big square robust head with a wide skull, muscular convex cheeks, strong wide jaws and deep mouth)

f) Cuello ancho, musculoso y corto (short wide muscular neck)

g) Pecho macizo, ancho, grande, profundo, costillas arqueadas y lomo musculado y corto (massive wide, deep chest with arched ribs and short muscled back)

h) Extremidades anteriores paralelas, rectas y robustas y extremidades posteriores muy musculosas, con patas relativamente largas formando un ángulo moderado (parallel, straight and robust extremities, very muscular, with relatively long legs forming a moderate angle)

The law also includes any dog that has shown aggressive behaviour to other dogs or humans and is considered by the authorities to be dangerous.

My dog is on the list, what do I have to do?

Each municipality of Spain have their infracciones of the laws, you should contact the local municipality and a Spanish vet to help understand the legal requirements for your dog for that particular area of Spain. You are looking for their information about "Perros Potencialmente Peligrosos" according to Ley 50/1999.

Attached below is a copy of **Ley 50/1999** and a computer generated translation together with the **Arrecife Infracciones** of this law that you can download or click the links to see them online.

You will be required to have a special licence "Licencia para la tenencia de animales potencialmente peligrosos" for this you have to be of legal age, without a criminal record (proof required from the Ministerio del Interior), have the physical and physiological ability to own a dangerous animal and an insurance policy covering the animal with a €120,000 liability.

Your dog will have to be registered with a local vet and have a micro chip, if you want to walk your dog outside the home they are expected to wear a muzzle, be kept on a secure lead no longer than 2 metres in length and only one dog per person. If the dog is kept outside at home, they must be secured and if lost reported to the local authorities within 48 hours. It is possible to take a test with a specially qualified vet to show your competence at controlling your dog and testing their aggression – if passed you will be given a certificate to prove the dog doesn't have to wear a muzzle outside the home.

There are two certificates issued by the local Ayuntamiento one is a permit to own a potentially dangerous dog, the other is to register your dog in the municipality. You need to take 2 photos of your dog, the dogs passport or book showing up to date vaccinations and micro chip details, your passport and Certificado de Residencia, proof of your non criminal record, insurance certificate for a liability of €120,000 for your dog. They will want to know why you have this type of dog, is it for personal defence, a guard dog or other reasons and if the dog has been trained the details of the trainer.

Cars

The ITV Test (MOT)

The ITV Test is a periodic test which motor vehicles must undergo in Spain. It is similar to the MOT test needed by cars in the United Kingdom. This article will take you through the ITV test requirements, and will show you how to book your own car in for an ITV in Lanzarote, and what to expect on the day.

ITV stands for Inspecion Technico Vehiculos, or technical inspection of vehicles. For most cars the test is due when they are four years old, and then once every two years. However, there are exceptions, notably commercial vehicles which have been converted to passenger use - for example the Citroen Berlingo, Renault Kangoo and Hyundai H1 - all of which require an ITV at two years of age. If in doubt, check your cars Ficha Technica document, which should be kept in the vehicle.

Booking an ITV is simple and the easiest way is to do so online. **http://www.serviciositv.es/**

On the appointed day, head to the ITV centre in Arrecife, which is just past the hospital on the San Bartolomé road. Go into the office with all the papers for your car and pay the fee, which ranges from €34 to €48 for a private car depending on whether it needs an emissions test and if it is petrol or diesel powered.. They will issue you with actual test form and direct you to the back of the building. If you have a diesel vehicle, you will first have to go into the diesel emissions' shed, which is the first building you will see. In there, they will ask you to step out of the car and the technician will plug the exhaust system into the computer and rev the engine. Once he has finished, head around the corner to the main building, where they will direct you into one of the lines and take your paperwork from you.

Basically, you are now on a kind of conveyor belt, and you will drive your car slowly to each station, where they will check, in turn:

Oil and water check
Lights, wipers, washers and horn function. Alignment of headlights, function of seat belts.
Emissions test (petrol cars)
Brakes and hand brake test
Inspection and test of tyres, shock absorbers, wheel cylinders, steering joints

At the last station, if your car has failed, you will be issued with a fail certificate with clear instructions on what need fixing. If your car has passed, the tester will fix a new sticker to the windscreen and hand back all your papers. Unless the car is more than 10 years old, the next test will be two years hence - if it is more than 10 years old, you will be expected to come back in a year, unless it's a commercial vehicle in which case it's every six months.

And that's it! Simple as you like and quite good fun!

Speeding Tickets

We've previously written information on **driving in Lanzarote** which details the local speed limits, traffic rules, parking and driving fines (multas), points system etc here in Lanzarote. Have you been unfortunate to be issued with a multa (fine)?

If you have a Spanish driving license and have received a multa then its now possible to pay them online with a debit or credit card (Visa / Master Card / Maestro).

* Go to the Dirección General de Tráfico website **www.dgt.es** and select the menu option on the left hand side called 'Trámites y Multas'.

* Next look for the heading '¿Alguna Multa?' select the single option "Pago de multas, notificationes, identificación de conductor, alegaciones, Centro de Denuncias Automatizadas.." underneath.

* Now you want the top option 'Pago de Multas' and select a) Pago de multas (sin certificado digital ni DNI electrónico).

* Enter the following details of your multa including the full amount of the fine, any discount will be calculated automatically for you. This information was requested in English! Document type, document number, first name, first surname, second surname, record or file number and total amount of the fine.

* Press continue and you will be prompted to enter your payment details and issued with a receipt.

You can still pay your fines in cash at the Jefatura de Tráfico in Arrecife, Banco Santander or the Correos as before and discounts are normally given if paid within 30 days of receiving your fine.

If you haven't been stopped by the police but believe that you may have been issued with a fine then you can use the following website to look for any outstanding multas. **www.buscamultas.com** is a free service provided by Dvuelta, they are warning drivers that the police no longer need to notify you of an offence and the first you may know about it is when an "embarga" is put on your bank account or your tax return! If you dispute the multa then you can contact Dvuelta for help to contest the fine.

Driving in Lanzarote

We've previously posted our **eight things to remember when you drive in Lanzarote** information but for those of you wanting a more detailed look at the rules for driving in Spain our full guide is below.

The Policía Municipal are responsible for traffic control within the towns, outside these areas it becomes the area of the Guardia Civil de Tráfico. The motorcycle police usually patrol in pairs and are trained in mechanics and first aid, they will stop and help any drivers in trouble. The police will often set up a check point and stop random motorists, they want to see your passport or residencia, driving license and vehicle registration papers (permiso de circulación) with insurance certificate (including proof of payment).

Speed limits in Lanzarote

Residential areas 20 kph

Built up areas 50 kph

Country roads 80 kph

Dual carriageways 100 kph

Traffic Fines

A traffic ticket (multa) issued should show the vehicle's registration number, details of the driver, details of the offence, police identification number and time limit for an appeal. Any non-resident driver will be asked to pay traffic fines on the spot and expect to be accompanied to a cash point if you don't have the funds on you! A resident is given 30 days to make the payment at a local bank or the tráfico office. A discount of up to 30% may offered for prompt or immediate payment, the fine is to be paid within 60 days otherwise.

The amount of the fine depends on the severity of the offence, they range up to €1,500.

Serious offences include driving at least 30 kph over the speed limit, driving whilst under the influence of drugs or alcohol, refusing to take a breathalyzer test, exceeding the number of people legally permitted in the vehicle.

Offences such as driving without lights, parking in a dangerous position, crossing a solid white line, driver or passengers not wearing a seatbelt carry fines from €91 to €300.

Minor offences such as using your mobile phone whilst driving, allowing a minor under the age of 12 in the front seat, carry a fine up to €90.

Click here for more information on how to **pay a multa online**.

Driving bans

Depending upon the severity of the traffic fine issued you may also receive a driving ban from 1-3 months. A driver who has been fined three times for serious offences within a two year period may have their license revoked.

Speed cameras

There is a fixed speed camera in Lanzarote, this is on the main dual carriage way from the Airport to Arrecife, the speed limit is 100 kph, the local police also have mobile speed cameras and can either pull you up at the scene to issue the ticket or you may only receive a notification in the post some weeks later.

Points

In Spain the driver starts with 12 points and a new driver with 8 points for their first three years. Points are deducted for traffic infractions along with the fine, if a driver loses all of their points, their license is revoked. Some examples of points taken for offences are:

6 points - drunk driving, refusing to take a breath test, driving at more than 150 per cent of the speed limit, dangerous driving

4 points - driving at more than 40kph over the limit, failing to stop at a red light or stop sign, throwing rubbish out of the car, dangerous overtaking

3 points - failing to maintain a safe distance behind the vehicle in front, driving between 30 and 40kph over the limit, driving without lights in poor visibility, using a hand-held mobile phone or wearing headphones while driving, not wearing a seatbelt (or helmet when riding a motorcycle)

2 points – stopping on a bend, driving between 20 and 30 kph over the limit

To regain a licence, drivers must retake the driving test and take a driving course of around 30 hours. These tests cannot be taken until at least six months after the last driving offence and can be taken only once every two years.

Liability

The owner of the car is liable for any offences relating to the vehicle such as the ITV and safety conditions.

The driver is responsible for the traffic violation, if the owner of the vehicle is notified about an offence where they were not driving, they should inform the police of the driver's details.

If the offender is under 18 years old, the parents or guardians are responsible for the fine, this would mainly applies to scooters as the legal age for driving a car is 18 in Spain.

Criminal Offences

Some traffic violations are also a criminal offence, such as driving whilst under the influence of drugs or alcohol, a car accident could be charged as homicide by misadventure, refusal to take a breathalyzer test and driving endangering other people. Generally the imprisonment term could be up to four years, lesser offences could be given a driving ban up to 10 years.

Seizing the Vehicle

The police have the rights to seize your car if it has been illegally parked or a non-resident driver refuses to pay the fine imposed, also if the car is immobile after an accident or it is believed to be abandoned.

Towing

You are not allowed to tow cars in Lanzarote, if your car breaks down or has an accident then you must call for a grúa (tow truck).

PLEASE NOTE OUR LATEST ARTICLE REFERRING TO THE **TRAFFIC LAW CHANGES ON THE 25TH MAY 2010**

Buying a car in Lanzarote

It's not as simple as you might think! The process is classically bureaucratic, but ultimately straightforward.

Where from?

The choice isn't as big as you might have thought, because most of the hire cars from here go back to be sold on the Spanish mainland. Most major manufacturers have dealers here, and they can be found in Arrecife, but very few of them offer second hand cars. Used cars tend to be left to the specialist used car dealers which can be found in Playa Honda and Arrecife.

One thing to note is that second hand values tend to be quite high here, as there is a demand for decent used cars. A late used car can make a new one seem a bargain!

Buying privately is pretty common, and you can find used cars for sale in The Gazette, Estohay magazine and online in classified adverts.

If you buy from a dealer, the "transferencia" will be taken care of normally as part of the price – that's changing the registration into your name. But if buying privately, you and the seller will have to do that job yourself. Here's the process:

Transferring a car from one owner to another

The seller must first visit his Ayuntamiento (town hall) to bring the road tax up to date, which will require payment. He or she will need the receipt for the next stage.

Both buyer and seller should then visit Registro de Propiedad on the Rambla Medular in Arrecife, with their photo identification documents and Certificados de Residencia, as well as the car documents – the ficha tecnica and the permiso de circulacion.

Before you get to registro, make photocopies of everything.

Tell the staff it's a vehicle change, and they will give you a copy of a sales contract (Contracto de compraventa), and a copy of the form they need to calculate the sales tax.

You should fill out both – the first is the contract to show who is selling the car, to whom, and for how much. The second is used for the tax, which is payable at the rate of 4% of the selling price. So for a €6000 car, you will have to pay €240 transfer tax. The buyer normally pays this, but it can be negotiated or even split.

Hand over all the forms and photocopies once your number is called, and the clerk will take your money and issue you with a copy of the transfer form, and also return all your original documents.

Trafico

The job isn't done yet!

Next you need to go to Jefatura local de Trafico (known as trafico), who are on Carretera Los Marmoles, opposite the petrol station, in Arrecife.

Once you get there, join the queue at the payment window on your left, and tell them you want to transfer a vehicle. They will take the money for a transfer (€50) and issue a receipt. Now you can take a number for the main windows.

Once your number is called, you have to take all your documents and the car documents, together with your receipt and the yellow form from registro to one of the main windows.

Here the clerk will check the documents, and then take the permiso de circulacion and issue a new one in the new owner's name.

At last, you're done!

More On Buying a car in Lanzarote

Used cars can be expensive in Lanzarote – it's simply a function of supply and demand. With a small population and therefore not many new cars being registered here each month, there's a limited choice. In UK, for example, there might be several thousand small hatchbacks for sale on any given day and all within a few hours drive. Here, there might only be a dozen!

And don't think all the hire cars add massively to the market – many are shipped off to the mainland when they come off hire.

It all adds up to it making sense to buy a new car, if you can afford to do so – not only are new cars cheaper here than in Northern Europe, you'll get more for it when you come to sell it!

Having said that, there are now some reasonable options when it comes to searching out second hand vehicles. Next to Mega Centro, and opposite Deiland, you'll find Multi Car and just along from there Autos Dibar, who sell off **Plus Car's ex rental cars**, which are generally in good condition. In Arrecife, you'll find The British Garage, and several small independent traders like Autos VIP, Sport Zentrum and Amicars.

There is a free publication called Motor 40, but the best place to seek out private sales is through the free magazine Estohay, or take a look at their website.

Preparation

Cars are rarely prepared well for sale here – quite often they are simply driven into the showroom and given a quick clean. On one hand that means you're seeing the car the way it really is, but on the other hand, you may be disappointed at how it looks!

Some garages will agree to doing some extra preparation work once the car is sold, for example a small repair, so always ask for it.

Warranty and Servicing

Many of the warranties given are pretty basic, and some only include parts, so be sure you know what you're getting with your purchase.

Trade Ins

Strangely very few companies offer any kind of trade-in service – so you'll often have to sell your own car before buying a new one. It's the weirdest thing, but something you just grow to live with. In my opinion, they are missing a valuable profit opportunity.

Negotiation

It's not normal to negotiate prices here for cars, and in many cases any attempt to do so will be greeted with a blank look and "The price is €xxxx!" It's always worth a try, but don't expect to get much of a deal.

Transferencia

There's a charge of 4% of the car's value, which is levied by Trafico, to transfer a car from one owner to another. Most dealers include this in the price, but always ask the question, particularly if buying privately.

Here a post that explains more: **Buying a car in Lanzarote**

ITV

Cars that are four years old require an ITV (Like and MOT) every two years, and once they are ten years old the requirement is every year. The ITV is displayed with a small sticker in the windscreen showing the expiry date.

Here's how to **ITV your car in Lanzarote**

Servicing

Garages often forget to stamp the servicing book, so when you do have your vehicle serviced, be sure to take it to reception with you, and insist on the official stamp.

Tyres

There are several tyre dealers on the island, in Arrecife, Playa Honda and Playa Blanca – it's worth getting comparative quotes from a couple – Lanzarote is hard on a car's tyres, with the hot tarmac and lack of rain, so you'll be buying tyres quite often.

Repairs

One issue we face here is that parts stocks tend to be quite low, so your car may be off the road for some time waiting for parts from the mainland. For that reason I'd recommend taking the option of a hire car when yours needs repair, through your insurance company, if that's available.

Road Tax

Road tax must be paid up to date in order for a car to be transferred to a new owner, so that always needs to be done, and your new tax, with your own local authority, will start from the day you take possession.

Utilities

Electricity

Unelco / Endesa have two offices in Lanzarote, the main office is situated in Arrecife on the main road from Tahiche, just past Eurospar there are two Shell garages on opposite sides of the road and the office is on the right just passed the garage. The smaller office is on the main high street in Tias, just along from the Maxcoop supermarket on the right before the end and the roundabout.

If you have purchased a property and need to change the billing details, you have to go in person or authorise someone to act on your behalf, they will want to see your escritura, identification, NIE/F number, bank account details and your contact address and phone number.

If you have any unpaid bills you cannot pay them at these offices, you need to take a special copy of the bill with a bar code on the bottom to your bank or local post office and payment can be made in cash. If you don't have a copy of the bill, you will need to go to Unelco and ask for a copy of the facturas pendiente first. If you have had your supply disconnected once paid, take your receipts back to the office and they will instruct an engineer to reconnect you within 24 hours of payment.

It is now possible to pay your bills over the phone with a credit card, this service is normally only available in Spanish, call the customer service line on 902 307 308 with your contracto number off your invoice.

The main Arrecife office is normally open from 9-4 Monday to Friday. The website for more information is **www.endesaonline.com**.

Water

It is now much easier to contact with Inalsa the local water company as their main office has moved from Calle Triana to the desalination plant in Costa Teguise, no more dashing around central Arrecife looking for a parking place! From the main road you turn into the entrance marked oficina and park on the right, go through the central door of the building on the left. Explain to the main on your left what you need - new connection, water disconnected, copy bill, change of ownership etc and he will issue you with a number and direct you to the correct desk.

If you find yourself in the unfortunate situation of having your water cut off for non-payment you will need to go to the Inalsa office with a copy bill or your Poliza number shown on previous bank payment receipts and pay the outstanding invoice plus a reconnection charge of 59.03 Euros. The water will be reconnected within 24 hours.

If you have purchased a property and want to change the ownership, you need to take a copy of the escritura, your NIE/F number, your empadronamiento certificate (if you want the discounted residents rate), your bank details for payment by direct debit and your address and contact telephone number.

The customer service number is 901 50 44 00. They have a website www.inalsa.es. The opening hours are:

From 16th September to 14th June
07:45 to 13:45 Monday to Thursday
07:45 to 12:45 Friday

From 15th June to the 15th September
07:45 to 12:45 Monday to Friday

What To Do In an emergency

Hopefully you won't need any of the following, but if you do need emergency numbers, help or advice whilst in Lanzarote here it is!

Emergency Telephone: (Police, Ambulance & Fire) 112

British Consulate & Embassy details for Lanzarote

Our British Consulate office is situated in Las Palmas, their contact details are:

Address: Calle Luis Morote 6-3º, 35007, Las Palmas de Gran Canaria

Telephone: 902 109 356 from within Spain or (0034) 91 334 2194 from outside Spain. NB. These are also the same numbers to contact the British Embassy based in Madrid.

Opening Hours: Tuesdays & Fridays 8.30am to 1.30pm

Website: **www.ukinspain.fco.gov.uk**

There is an Emergency Consular Team based in London, their office is manned 24 hours per day telephone: (0044) 020 7008 1500.

Lost or Stolen Passport in Lanzarote

If you have lost or had your passport stolen you need to report it to the local Policía Nacional as soon as possible. If you can't speak Spanish you will need to have a translator to make the report, they will then issue you with a police report. If you need an urgent replacement for your passport then contact the consulate in Las Palmas who will arrange for the honorary consul to issue you a travel document. If you are living in Lanzarote or have more than 4 weeks before your next travel then you can apply for a replacement via the British Embassy in Madrid.

The passport forms can be downloaded direct from **British Embassy in Madrid** we have attached the current forms below but please check that these are still valid before posting to Madrid.

Once you have the forms completed (LS01 & C1 for an adult) you will require 2 identical passport photos, these can be provided in the correct format by the Kodak shop on the ground floor of the Deiland Shopping Centre in Playa Honda, the original of your police report, other documents required such as birth certificate and the correct fee.

An adult's passport (32 page) currently costs €152 and child's €97 plus a courier charge of €16 per household to the Canary Islands. An emergency travel document is €109 if issued during normal opening hours and an additional €157 call out fee if outside normal hours.

Passport helpline (premium rate number €1.16/min) 807 450 051.

Post to the British Embassy addressed to UK Regional Passport Processing Centre, British Consulate-General, Torre Espacio, Paseo de la Castellana 259D, 28046, Madrid.

Death of a UK Citizen in Lanzarote

It is Spanish law that a body must be preserved or embalmed within 48 hours of death. The next of kin will be informed by the authorities to find out if the body is being repatriated to the UK or if there will be a local burial / cremation.

If the deceased is covered by travel insurance the insurers need to be notified immediately, they will make arrangements with a local funeral director to repatriate the body. A special casket is required for the transport along with certificates for the death, embalming and permission to transport the body, arrangements will take 8-10 days.

If the decision is for a local burial or cremation then the next of kin need to contact a local funeral director to make the arrangements. A burial in Spain is normally above ground, the body is placed in a crypt for 5 years unless purchased in perpetuity. Cremations are now more popular and it is much easier to make arrangements to transport the ashes back to the UK. Please note that airline regulations stipulate that ashes must be transported in the cargo hold.

Police in Lanzarote

There are three different police organisations in Spain, all of them are armed. The traffic is monitored by two different police, the Policía Municipal are responsible for traffic control within the towns, outside these areas it becomes the area of the Guardia Civil de Tráfico, for more information please read our article on **driving in Lanzarote**.

Policía Guardia Civil

Website: www.guardiacivil.org

Telephone: 062

Local Direct Telephone No's: Costa Teguise 928 592 400, San Bartolomé 928 520 711, Teguise 928 800 847, Tías 928 510 336, Yaiza 928 830 117, Tráfico 928 811 886.

The Civil Guard are responsible for national security they wear a green uniform. The Guardia Civil carry out duties for the Ministry of Defence and the Interior Ministry to protect the public's safety, Spain's borders (ports, airports, coastal and land), environmental laws and police traffic.

Policía Nacional

Website: www.policia.es

Telephone: 092

Local Direct Telephone No's: Arrecife 928 811 317, Haría 928 835 252, San Bartolomé 928 520 712, Teguise 928 845 252, Tías 928 834 101, Tinajo 928 840 729, Yaiza 928 830 107.

The National Police (Cuerpo Nacional de Policía) are responsible for criminal investigations, immigration and identification, they wear either a black or blue uniform. This is the police station if you need to report a crime (denuncia) you can call 902 102 112 for more information, you will have to visit in person to make a report and have a translator with you if you can't speak Spanish.

Policía Municipal

Telephone: 091

The Municipality Police (Policía Local) are responsible to the mayor and ayuntamiento in each local municipality, they take responsibility for local traffic control, minor offences and wear a blue and white uniform.

Useful Emergency Phrases

Help – socorro

Can you help me – puede ayudarme

Where is the police station – dónde está la comisaría

I need a report for my insurance – necesito un informe para el seguro

I want to report a theft – quiero denunciar un robo

Other Useful Emergency Numbers:

928 846 001 - Arrecife Airport

928 811 546 – Arrecife Bus Station (Estación de Guaguas)

928 816 312 - Arrecife Fire Station

928 595 000 – Arrecife General Hospital

928 810 100 – Cabildo de Lanzarote

928 812 222 – Cruz Roja (Red Cross)

012 – Doctors Appointment

620 896 185 – Locksmith (Brian from Lanzalocks)

900 202 202 – Seguridad Marítima

1004 – Telefonica (phone company)

928 597 292 – Grúa (breakdown recovery)

901 504 400 – Inalsa (Cliente) Water Company Customer Service

901 514 400 – Inalsa (Averías) Water Company Emergency Alert

902 519 519 – Unelco Endesa (Averías) Electric Company Emergency Alert

902 508 850 – Unelco Endesa (Cliente) Electric Company Customer Service

676 455 282 – Translator and Paperwork Advice (Guy Buske from A-Z Paperwork)

928 804 153 – Lawyer (Maria José Pérez Callero)

928 520 176 – Taxi (Lanzarote Taxi)

928 810 305 - Tahiche Prison (El Centro Penitenciario de Arrecife)

Medical Emergency

If you're just feeling unwell and need medicine or general advice then seek the help of the local pharmacy, they are very good and usually speak English. Drugs are readily available over the counter, this is the only place you can buy pain relief such as Nurofen or Paracetamol and normally come in boxes of 600mg tablets so check the dosage. Antibiotics are now only available by prescription. A list of duty pharmacies can be found on **www.farmacias-lanzarote.es**

You should be travelling with your European Health Insurance Card (EHIC) this together with your passport will entitle you to the equivalent of the NHS service here in Spain, you can't use the local Centro de Salud (Doctors) but will be seen at the **General Hospital José Molina Orosa** in Arrecife for any necessary treatment during your stay.

For those with private health insurance or travel insurance there are an abundance of private clinics within each of the resorts for treatment and the private hospital Hospiten situated on the outskirts of Puerto del Carmen.

Here are some handy phrases for the pharmacy just in case....

Have you something for – tiene algo para....

Toothache – dolor de muelas

Insect bites – picaduras

Stomach ache – dolor de estómago

Food poisoning – intoxicación alimenticia

Headache – dolor de cabeza

Sunburn – quemaduras del sol

Pregnant – embarazada

Schooling and Kids

Types of school

There are three types of school on the Island: local Spanish, Private English, and Private International.

The private option is expensive (approx 4000€ per annum per child dependant on age). This may be a good option for your children if any of the following apply:
- Your children are of secondary school age
- You are only intending to live in Lanzarote for a year or two
- You want your children to be taught the UK curriculum and obtain GCSEs and A Levels

Local Spanish schools obviously teach in Spanish, and qualifications obtained enable kids to go on to university, technical education and training on the Island and in Spain. This may be a good option if:
- Your children are of primary school age
- You want your children to be fluent in Spanish
- You intend to remain on the island for the long term
- You want your children to obtain qualifications relevant to further education on the island / mainland Spain.

Private School Options

The British school of Lanzarote (Tahiche)
This is pronominally Spanish pupils having an English education. The school is small and the class sizes are small and teaching is personally geared towards each pupil. There is a school uniform at this school.

Collegio Hispano Britanico (Puerto del Carmen)
This mainly English pupils getting an English education. The standard is quite high and aimed at getting pupils into higher (University) education. It is a large school. There is no uniform. The school is quite focussed on sport and has several teams that complete with other schools around the Canaries.

Centro Educacional Daos (Matagorda)
This is a trilingual school (English, Spanish and German). It has a uniform. It opened in 2007. It has a different approach to the other schools in that the teachers rotate, and the children stay in the same classroom, the lessons are taught in a rotation of the 3 languages.

Collegio Arenas International (Costa Teguise)
It is part of a group of school in the Canaries Islands. There is a school uniform. Classes are held in Spanish and in English. There is a lot of after school activities on offer.

State School Know How

You need to prove you live in the local area (by showing your Empadronmiento certificate). There are some forms to fill in and paperwork that the school will want to have copies of (passports, medical records (especially vaccination records), passport photos (Spanish size), and birth certificates). They will also ask for your previous years tax return, but if you are new to the island you won't have one, so they will accept your children and wait for this to be supplied later. You may need to supply a certificate from the Island Tax Office stating you haven't earned on the island in the previous year. They will also usually wait for your social security number as you need a job with a contract to get one.

If your local school has no places in your child's year, then you will offered a place at the next nearest school with space.

Most of the local schools do not require a uniform, but some have an optional one. Text and exercise books are expected to be purchased by the parents at the beginning of each school year (September).

The hours of local schools are typically:
Primary 9 - 1
Secondary 8 - 2

They take a snack for the morning break, and lunch is eaten at home.

If you live more than 3Km from the nearest school your child is entitled to a free place on the school bus (subject to availability) which has certain pick up and drop off points in the area.

Our more detailed post on the nursery and school options can be found here - **Schools in Lanzarote**

British School of Lanzarote
Calle Juan Echevarria
35509
Tahiche
Telephone & Fax: (0034) 928 810 085
Web link for more

information: http://www.thebritishschoollanzarote.com/

Colegio Arenas International
Avenida del Mar 37
35509
Costa Teguise
Telephone: (0034) 928 590 835
http://www.colegioarenas.es/htmlengl/contactar/admisiones.htm

Colegio Hispano Britanico
Cno Mosefue 2
Teguise
Telephone: (0034) 928 173 066
Web link for more information:http://www.colegiohispanobritanico.com

Colegio Europeo Daos
Marte No 3
Puerto del Carmen
Telephone: 928 51 58 18
http://www.colegioeuropeodaos.com

Spanish Schools List
Web link: http://www.lawebdelanzarote.com/educacion/centros.htm

More on Schools in Lanzarote

For those parents enrolling children for the first time, here is our Lanzarote Information guide to the nurseries, primary schools, secondary schools and further education available on the island. For the right to a state school place you must have residencia and a certificado de empadronamiento which proves your entitlement as a Spanish resident and the municipality you reside in.

School education is compulsory in Spain for children aged from 6 to 16 years old, Educación Primaria is the primary school for children from 6 – 11 years of age and Educación Secundaria Obligatoria is the secondary school for 12 – 15 year olds. There are two kinds of pre schools a Jardin de Infancia / Guardería takes babies up to 3 years and Educación Infantil from 3 to 5 years old.

Nursery / Jardin de Infancia / Guardería

The nurseries take babies from 0 – 3 years old, these are generally private and fee paying and aim to develop a toddler's physical and mental skills and by the age of three they are learning their alphabet and to read & write.

Arrecife:

E.E.I. Sanjurjo Meneje C/ Rafael s/n, 35500, Arrecife, Lanzarote

Tel: 928 81 55 75

Guardería Dumbo C/ Figueroa 15, 35500, Arrecife, Lanzarote

Tel: 928 81 48 04

Jardin de Infancia el Duende C/ Víctor Hugo 50, 35500, Arrecife, Lanzarote

Tel: 928 80 76 90

Minicole C/ Méjico 66, 35500, Arrecife, Lanzarote

Tel: 928 81 70 23

Pilar Garcia Piño C/ Jose Ortega y Gasset 51, 35500, Arrecife, Lanzarote

Telephone: (0034) 928 815 912

Haría:

Guardería Municipal Plaza de la Constitución, nº 10, 35520, Haría, Lanzarote

Tel: 928 83 54 26

San Bartolomé:

Disney C/ Cordel 10-B, 35509, San Bartolomé, Lanzarote

Tel: 928 82 10 29

Nanny C.C. Chimidas, C/ Navío, loc.15-16, Playa Honda, 35509, San Bartolomé, Lanzarote

Tel: 928 82 30 84

Teguise:

Compiguarde S.L. C/ Acacias s/n, Costa Teguise, 35508, Lanzarote

Tel: (0034) 928 826 618

Guarderias Infantiles Av. Bungavillas 16, Costa Teguise, 35508, Teguise, Lanzarote

Tel: 928 591 308

Tías:

Guardería Popito S.Cv.P C/ Reyes Católicos 26, 35572, Tías, Lanzarote

Tel: 928 83 41 22

Jardin de Infancia C/ Marte 3, 35510, Puerto del Carmen, Tías, Lanzarote

Tel: 928 51 42 69 / 928 515 818

Yaiza:

Guarderías Infantiles C/ Francia (Urb. Virginia Oasis) s/n, 35580, Playa Blanca, Yaiza, Lanzarote

Tel: 928 519 752

Guarderías Infantiles Av. Femés 25, 35570, Yaiza, Lanzarote

Tel: 928 518 899

Primary School / Educación Infantil / Educación Primaria/ Colegios Infantiles

Educación Infantil or pre school education for children aged from 3 to 5 years old is offered at most primary schools but not compulsory. Educación Primaria or primary school is for children aged from 6 to 11 years old, there are three stages each lasting two years the children are taught in Spanish including subjects of math, history, geography, biology, sport and a second language depending upon the school, this could be English, French or German. Catholic religion classes are offered but can be opted out for alternative studies. Each pupil needs to pass the second year of each of the stages or they may be asked to repeat a year to ensure they have understood the course before advancing to the next level. Hours can vary but typically from 9am to 1pm unless the school has comedor when they can be extended until 4pm. You will be issued with a list of materials and text books which you are expected to provide each September when the new school year starts, budget around €150 per child plus school uniform if the school has one as not all of them do.

Arrecife:

CEIP Adolfo Topham C/ Doctor Gómez Ulla 71, Arrecife, Lanzarote

Tel: 928 800 181

CEIP Antonio Zerolo C/ Guenia 3, Arrecife, Lanzarote

Tel: 928 813 659

CEIP Argana Alta C/ Campoamor 14, Arrecife, Lanzarote

Tel: 928 816 731 / 928 807 689

CEIP Benito Méndez Tarajano C/ Severo Ochoa 29, Arrecife, Lanzarote

Tel: 928 810 204

CEIP Capellanía del Yágabo C/ Severo Ochoa s/n, Arrecife, Lanzarote

Tel: 928 814 212

CEIP La Destila C/ Eugenio D'Ors 2, Arrecife, Lanzarote

Tel: 928 805 256

CEIP Los Geranios C/ Mosta 1, Urb. Los Geranios, Arrecife, Lanzarote

Tel: 928 810 235

CEIP Mercedes Medina Díaz C/ Mosta 5, Urb. Los Geranios, Arrecife, Lanzarote

Tel: 928 811 799

CEIP Nieves Toledo C/ El Indio 19, Arrecife, Lanzarote

Tel: 928 813 432

CEIP Titerroy C/ Tilama 1, Arrecife, Lanzarote

Tel: 928 810 959 / 928 807 379

Haría:

CEIP La Garita C/ La Marina s/n, Arrieta, Haría, Lanzarote

Tel: 928 848 021

CEIP Las Mercedes C/ Villa Nueva 8, Mala, Haría, Lanzarote

Tel: 928 829 617

CEIP San Juan C/ Santiago Noda 4, Haría, Lanzarote

Tel: 928 835 111

San Bartolomé:

CEIP Ajei C/ Constitución 9, San Bartolomé, Lanzarote

Tel: 928 520 328

CEIP El Quintero C/ General Franco s/n, San Bartolomé, Lanzarote

Tel: 928 520 666

CEIP Güime La Carretera s/n, Gúime, San Bartolomé, Lanzarote

Tel: 928 821 224

CEIP María Auxiliadora C/ Lomo Tesa 40, Montaña Blanca, San Bartolomé, Lanzarote

Tel: 928 820 928

CEIP Playa Honda C/ San Borondón s/n, Playa Honda, San Bartolomé

Tel: 928 823 386 / 928 819 159

Teguise:

CEIP César Manrique Cabrera C/ Rafael Alberti s/n, Tahiche, Teguise, Lanzarote

Tel: 928 843 477

CEIP Costa Teguise C/ Malagueña s/n, Costa Teguise, Teguise, Lanzarote

Tel: 928 346 647 / 638 749 383

CEIP Doctor Alfonso Spínola C/ Garajonay s/n, Villa de Teguise, Teguise, Lanzarote

Tel: 928 845 042

CEIP Guenia C/ Tanausú 10, Guatiza, Teguise, Lanzarote

Tel: 928 529 408 / 928 529 717

CEIP La Caleta de Famara La Caleta, Caleta de Famara, Teguise, Lanzarote

Tel: 928 528 698

CEIP Los Valles C/ Arrorró 4, Los Valles, Teguise, Lanzarote

Tel: 928 528 022

CEIP Muñique C/ La Era 12, Muñique, Teguise, Lanzarote

Tel: 928 529 132

CEIP Nazaret Las abubillas 4, Nazaret, Teguise, Lanzarote

Tel: 928 845 397

CEIP Soo C/ San Juan Evangelista 157, Soo, Teguise, Lanzarote

Tel: 928 526 135

CEIP Tao C/ Tagarifo 25, Tao, Teguise, Lanzarote

Tel: 928 529 270

CEIP Teseguite C/ Brega 1, Teseguite, Teguise, Lanzarote

Tel: 928 845 785

CEIP Tiagua C/ Achamán 31, Tiagua, Teguise, Lanzarote

Tel: 928 529 812

Tías:

CEIP Alcalde Rafael Cedrés C/ Igualdad 5, Tías, Lanzarote

Tel: 928 833 488

CEIP Concepción Rodríguez Artiles C/ Terrero 2, Puerto del Carmen, Tías, Lanzarote

Tel: 928 811 648

CEIP La Asomada Carretera General 23, La Asomada, Tías, Lanzarote

Tel: 928 834 198

Tinajo:

CEIP El Cuchillo El Cuchillo 21, Tinajo

Tel: 928 840 574

CEIP Guiguan C/ Agua Clara 2, Mancha Blanca, Tinajo, Lanzarote

Tel: 928 840 214

CEIP Liria La Vegueta La Vegueta 163, Tinajo, Lanzarote

Tel: 928 838 028

CEIP Virgen de Los Volcanes Avda de Los Volcanes 54, Tinajo, Lanzarote

Tel: 928 840 042 / 928 838 103

Yaiza:

CEIP Las Breñas C/ Plaza San Luis 4, Las Breñas, Yaiza, Lanzarote

Tel: 928 830 242

CEIP Mararía Avda el Rubicón 12, Femés, Yaiza, Lanzarote

Tel: 679 453 863

CEIP Playa Blanca Urb, Montaña Roja, Parcela 69, Playa Blanca, Yaiza, Lanzarote

Tel: 928 517 541

CEIP Uga C/ Uga 38, Uga, Yaiza, Lanzarote

Tel: 928 836 216

CEIP Yaiza El Barranco 1, Yaiza, Lanzarote

Tel: 928 836 208

Secondary School / Instituto /Educación Secundaria Obligatoria (ESO)

Children from the age of 12 to 15 are required to attend a secondary school or Instituto as they are known locally. The classes are called ESO with first, second, third and fourth years. There are exams each term with reports and parents evening so that you know how your child is progressing through the year, the subjects are graded up to a score of 10 with 5 or more a pass. As in primary school your child may be asked to repeat a year or recuperate during the summer holidays if they haven't passed the grades. When a pupil reaches their 16th birthday they can leave school without qualification or continue until they have completed the full school course and earned their secondary education certificate which is equivalent to the GCSE qualifications. Hours are from 8am to 2pm and again you will be expected to provide text books and materials each year.

Arrecife:

IES Agustín Espinosa C/ Coronel Bens 7, Arrecife, Lanzarote

Tel: 928 811 169

IES Arrecife Barriada San Francisco Javier, Arrecife, Lanzarote

Tel: 928 806 090 / 928 801 897

IES Blas Cabrera Felipe C/ Alcalde Ginés de La Haz 57, Arrecife, Lanzarote

Tel: 928 805 960

IES César Manrique C/ Doctor Puigvert s/n, Arrecife, Lanzarote

Tel: 928 812 344 / 928 812 237

IES Las Salinas C/ Tamaragua 2, Arrecife, Lanzarote

Tel: 928 814 675 / 928 813 969

IES Zonzamas C/ Doctor Barraquer 6, Arrecife, Lanzarote

Tel: 928 813 114 / 928 813 052

Haría:

IES Haría C/ Santiago Noda 4, Haría, Lanzarote

Tel: 928 835 057

San Bartolomé:

IES Playa Honda C/ Mástil s/n, Playa Honda, San Bartolomé, Lanzarote

Tel: 928 819 052

IES San Bartolomé Carretera General Arrecife Tinajo s/n, San Bartolomé, Lanzarote

Tel: 928 520 984 / 928 521 399

Teguise:

IES Teguise C/ Gadifer de La Salle 23, Villa de Teguise, Teguise, Lanzarote

Tel: 928 845 471 / 928 845 613

Tías:

IES Puerto del Carmen Rambla Islas Canarias 39, Puerto del Carmen, Tías, Lanzarote

Tel: 928 513 425

IES Tías C/ Tajinaste s/n, Camino de Los Lirios, Tías, Lanzarote

Tel: 928 834 383

Tinajo:

IES Tinajo C/ Montaña Tenesar 1, El Calvario, Tinajo, Lanzarote

Tel: 928 838 096

Yaiza:

IES Yaiza C/ Mácher s/n, Yaiza, Lanzarote

Tel: 928 512 102 / 928 512 103

Private Schools in Lanzarote

There is currently a choice of four private schools in Lanzarote based in Puerto del Carmen, Costa Teguise and Tahiche. Expect to pay fees in the region of €1300 per child per term, they each offer different services and types of schooling.

British School of Lanzarote Calle Juan Echevarria, 35507, Tahiche, Lanzarote

Tel: 928 810 085

Pupils from 3-16 years old, classes are taught in English following the British National Curriculum.

Colegio Arenas International Avenida del Mar 37, 35508, Costa Teguise, Lanzarote

Tel: 928 590 835

Pupils from 2-18 years old, classes are taught 50% Spanish 50% English following the Spanish curriculum.

Colegio Hispano Británico Situated behind Rancho Texas, Puerto del Carmen, 35510, Tías, Lanzarote

Tel: 928 173 066

Pupils from nursery to sixth form, classes taught in English following the British National Curriculum.

Centro Educacional Daos C/Marte 3, Matagorda, 35510, Puerto del Carmen, Tías, Lanzarote

Tel: 928 515 818

Pupils from 3 months -11 years old, all classes are taught in three languages equally Spanish, English & German.

Further Education

A levels are possible at Colegio Hispano Británico, for children educated in Spanish they have the following options:

Professional training – Formación Profesional

Available at IES Arrecife, IES Blas Cabrera Felipe, IES César Manrique, IES Zonzamas, IES Haría, IES Teguise (details above)

IFPMP Arrecife (maritime) Avda Naos 2, Arrecife, Lanzarote Tel: 928 810 600

General education – Bachillerato

Bachillerato is the equivalent to A Level education and the path to attending University (plus the entrance exam Prueba de Acceso). This is a two year course taught in Spanish with a second foreign language, philosophy, physical education, history and one of these options:

Art: History of art, sculpture & painting

Nature & Sciences: Biology, chemistry, physics including math

Sciences & Engineering: Physics, math, chemistry including technical drawing

Humanities: Latin, Greek, history of art

Available at IES Agustín Espinosa, IES Arrecife, IES Blas Cabrera Felipe, IES César Manrique, IES Las Salinas, IES Zonzamas, IES Haría, IES Playa Honda,

IES San Bartolomé, IES Teguise, IES Tías, IES Tinajo & IES Yaiza (details above)

EA Pancho Lasso (art), C/ Travesía de Alfredo Kraus 1, Arrecife, Lanzarote Tel: 928 811 650

Information from the Gobierno de Canarias & Consejería de Educación can be found on this link **Spanish Education in the Canary Islands**.

Special Educational Needs in Lanzarote

Special educational needs are not something that the education system in any one country has ever got 100% accurate. There is always a margin of error as not everyone with SEN has the same diagnosis, and not everyone who has the same diagnosis has the same symptoms. Complicated!

So by taking a personal look at the Spanish education system I see many areas where improvements could and should be made, especially for children with autistic spectrum disorders (ASD) and those who suffer from language and communication disorders as well as children with dyslexia and many areas where the Spanish education system is actually more defined than the UK by learning methods rather than by achieving status and goal setting.

Apart from there being a free (other than stationery supplies) education for children who are residents of Lanzarote in the public schools, the system itself is remarkable in the way it focuses primarily on the child and the child's achievements rather than in assessments and target setting. There may or may not be a uniform (school dependent), lessons are morning based with children mostly being home by 1.30pm unless there are specified afternoon activities or your child attends a local private school which usually operate until 4pm and costs approx €4000p.a The Spanish education system also follows a policy of exams and grades being passed before the child can progress into the next academic year.

This type of education system is perfect for children with learning disabilities as it focuses on core subjects early in the day when the brain is most active and most receptive to learning. By mid-afternoon when children with LD become more obviously tired and sluggish the school day is over or the activities change.

The Spanish education act (LOE) encourages the school system to cater for children with special needs within the mainstream schools and only advocates the use of specials schools if the child cannot be taught or the school cannot adapt to meet the needs of the child without massive structural alteration of the building or unless the child is deemed to be a danger to other students. This type of inclusion policy can be beneficial if the school and the special needs co-ordinator, child, parent and special teaching assistant can all work together to provide excellent teaching methods, teaching apparatus and specialist learning materials that encourage the child to learn and achieve its potential without causing disruption to the class and to the child itself.

For children with dyslexia it may mean that the parents would have to pay for extra books and learning materials to support their child if the school does not provide any extra support. This could also mean that the child may struggle if Spanish is his/her second language. Extra tuition or spending extra time at home on reading and self help techniques to support sight reading and word recognition are important parts of the dyslexia curriculum support package. By meeting with the school and with teachers to work on an agreed format to support the child parents and teachers can strive to improve academic performance. It may also mean that the child is likely to repeat the academic year until the specific grade requirements are met.

For children with autistic spectrum disorders and language and communication disorders it is imperative that they are assessed correctly and get the specialised help that they are going to need. This will be in the form of a socialised support assistant who can provide 1-2-1 support throughout the school day. The child is likely to need help with social skills, learning support, language development and help with playtime and transitions from lessons.

Extra support needed for ASD children would include a visual time-table, PECS cards in either English or Spanish, social stories implementation, behaviour charts (5-point scale) and further academic support material.

The need for inclusion for a child with ASD is dependent upon the severity of the child and the support and integration put in place within early years settings and early education. It is very evident that teachers and parents will be spending a lot of time working closely to achieve a good inclusion policy and setting in motion specialist provision for language therapy, individual education plans, occupational therapy (Spanish equivalent) and providing positive behavioural rewards. Provided the right amount of help can be provided and the child is encouraged and rewarded for behaviour and learning the inclusion can be extremely worthwhile.

A child with ASD is extremely likely to need to repeat academic years on more than one occasion throughout his/her schooling.

Shopping in Lanzarote

Food Shopping

The food shops in Lanzarote fall conveniently into four categories:

Tourist Supermarkets
These are based in the resorts and are usually either Netto, HiperDino or Marcial owned. Prices are normally higher, but there is a good selection of international products and they usually have the best selection of booze and tobacco products. Convenient, but costly.

Residential Supermarkets
This sector now consists of the following supermarkets in Lanzarote:

Eurospar Arrecife
Eurospar Costa Teguise
Eurospar Macher
HiperDino Deiland Playa Honda
HiperDino (ex Vivo) Playa Honda
HiperDino Arrecife
HiperDino Playa Blanca
Lidl Arrecife

These are aimed at locals and are much more keenly priced. All have meat and delicatessen counters and a good selection of product, although the goods for sale are skewed towards the Spanish eating style.

These are your best options for finding **baby products in Lanzarote**.

Into this category, we would also add Congelados Roper who have **supermarkets in Playa Blanca**, Tías and **Playa Honda**. They are a frozen food, fresh fruit and vegetable store in Playa Honda, which is terrific value for money. **Congelados AfricaMar** have shops in Playa Honda, San Bartolomé & Arrecife and offer high quality, frozen fish, meat and vegetables from local suppliers. **El Huerto** are a fantastic chain of fruit and vegetable shops in Lanzarote.

Local Food Shops

These are out of the resorts and have a limited choice, but can be surprisingly cheap. Places like the fruit and vegetable shop and butchers at Valterra in Arrecife, the garage (yes really!) in Arrieta, and all the other little "Auto Servicios" (self service mini markets) you will see on your travels. Try them you'll be surprised!

Specialist Food Shops

There are any number of these on the island and within them we would include the "English" supermarkets such as **Gangas Outlet** and Maceys in Tias. They stock imported British goods and are the only place you are likely to be able to buy things like horse radish or Oxo cubes and other strangely British stuff!

There is also a **Chinese supermarket** in Arrecife, and the **Yash Supermarket** in Puerto del Carmen, which sells all kinds of Indian spices and food.

There are a number of places where you can buy **gluten free products in Lanzarote**, some supermarkets stock basic ranges with more specialist ranges available in the health food shops.

Shopping Centres

Biosfera Plaza Shopping Centre

The Biosfera Plaza Centre is situated on Calle Juan Carlos I over looking the Old Town of **Puerto del Carmen**. The building is modern with large sails for shade on the top floors, there is parking below the building and the bus stop is right outside with a taxi rank next door. There is a good selection of shops, mainly clothes such as Zara, Pimkie, Crocs, Quiksilver, Oyosho, Natural Shop, Pull and Bear, Levi's. Not to mention the perfume shop, Calzados - a great shoe shop, sports clothes shop, Informatica - stationery and phone shop, amusement arcade and bars / restaurants for relaxing in and enjoying the panoramic sea views. The opening hours are from 10:00am to 22:00pm Monday to Saturday and reduced opening hours on a Sunday.

Deiland Shopping Centre

The Deiland Centre in Playa Honda was the first large indoor shopping centre on the island. The centre is visible from the main dual carriage road running from Arrecife towards Playa Blanca so is easy to find and there is parking outside or underneath the building. Inside on the ground floor you will find a large Hiperdino supermarket, Lolita the bakery, Imaginarium which is similar to the Early Learning Centre, Burbujita a great sports shop, an opticians, a selection of clothes and shoe shops including the fashion chain stradivarius, Tom Jones and Quiksilver, a lovely house and gift shop, the lottery office and some great coffee bars. On the lower floor there is Bricoland a DIY shop, a large toy shop with a baby equipment area, pet shop, book shop and luna records. On the top floor is a large Sony electrical shop, Informatica the stationers and mobile phone shop, a bowling alley, cinema, Burger King and KFC (Kentucky Fried Chicken)!! On the back plaza of Deiland there are a couple of bars and restaurants, L'Opera is a minutes walk away and there is a Scruples shop for English bedding just to the side of the centre. More information on their website **www.deilandplaza.com**

Shopping in Arrecife

Many people are daunted by the thought of a shopping trip into Arrecife, the capital of Lanzarote - but don't be! Yes there are one way systems but there is plenty of parking and lots on offer, so have a go, but remember the shops close for siesta in the afternoon, so arrive at 10am or 5pm for a leisurely wander with no time constraints.

If its your first time into Arrecife, its probably best to tackle it by heading for the Gran Hotel, there is always parking available underneath and you can see it as a landmark if you get lost! If approaching from the airport side of the capital, take the right hand lane at the end of the dual carriageway but head to your left along the beach and seafront, the car park entrance is on the roundabout in front of you. If approaching from Costa Teguise, go straight across at the funny junction – taking care to stop where required and look in the right direction, just before Ikea there is a turning on the left to the **Castillo San José,** take this old coast road to the roundabout with the fishermen on, straight over past the big boat shops, bear to the left at the mini roundabout and again at the next one and you will circle around Charco San Ginés along the front, when you see the Gran Hotel, take the exit for the underground car park off the roundabout.

If you're confident driving around Arrecife the most central multi storey car park is the one at the Spinola Boulevard, or the one just before Casa on Calle Fajardo.

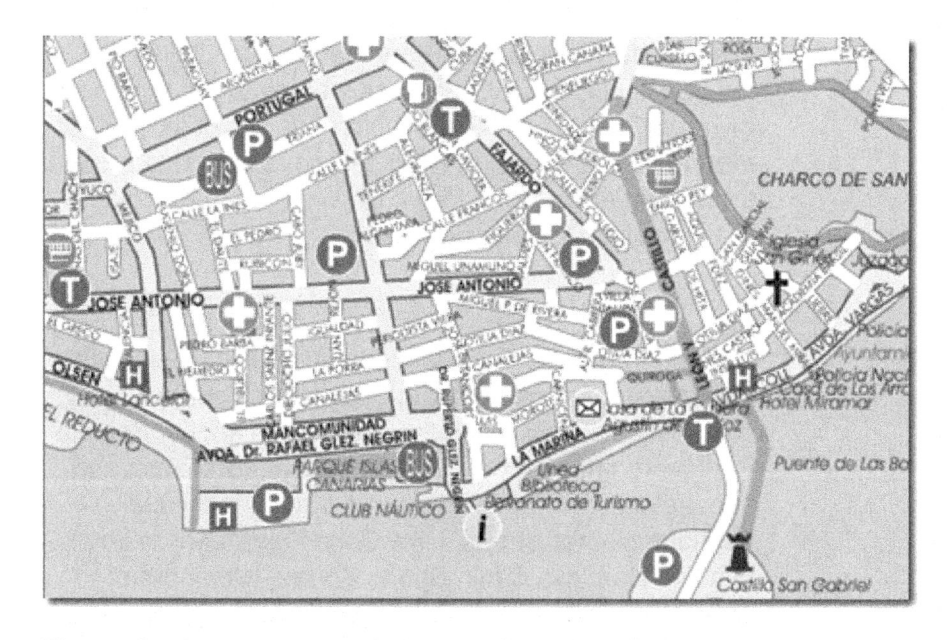

The main shopping street is León y Castillo or Calle Real as its known locally, this is a pedestrianised area, the easiest way to find it is to walk along the front with the Gran Hotel and beach behind you along the promenade until you see the Puente de las Bolas drawbridge and the **Castillo de San Gabriel** on your right, the road that leads out to them is Calle Real, simply follow this to the left and you're on the main street. In Calle Real you will find lots of branches of the local banks, clothes shops such as Mango, Zara, Vera Moda, Jack Jones, a variety of shoe shops, perfumes, tobacco specialist, bargain euro or Chinese shops, there is even a department store.

Wander down the side streets that lead off Calle Real, if the sea is behind you, the ones leading to the right head towards Charco San Ginés which has lots of little boats moored and a selection of cafés and restaurants around the waters edge, don't forget to pop into the **Recova market** which is open until 2pm.

On the left of Calle Real you can find La Plazuela with Mothercare, Animal, Rip Curl, Benetton, designer sunglasses shops, jewellers, more shoe shops. Spinola Boulevard offers, a café, book shop, hairdressers, surf shop, electical shop. There are plenty of individual boutique clothes shops, I like Calle Fajardo, here you can find Barclays Bank, Sports Zone – two floors of sporting clothes and accessories, Casa - a great house and gift shop, children's clothes, more shoe shops, stationery etc etc.

I always find there's a great atmosphere around Arrecife, people are stopping in the streets to chat with friends, lots of little cafés, nooks and crannies to explore!

Christmas Shopping in Lanzarote

Residents of Lanzarote already know where to buy their Christmas goodies but for those of you who have recently **relocated** to the island or just coming for a Christmas **holiday** here are some suggestions of where to find all the trimmings to make your Christmas festive in Lanzarote.

Food

A lot of your Christmas shopping can be condensed into a visit to a couple of shops in Lanzarote, I haven't mentioned items that can now be found regularly at the local Spanish supermarkets such as pork pies, pickles, relishes, tins of chocolates and British cheeses.

Turkeys can be found in the frozen section of the larger local supermarkets, there are also fresh turkey breasts available off the butchers counter, I have already seen them on sale in Eurospar and Ropers.

Cranberry sauce used to be a British supermarket item only but I bought it recently in the Eurospar La Lonja near Puerto del Carmen, its on the top shelf of the second to last isle on the far end.

Stuffing is only available from British supermarkets, something I buy on a visit to the **Gangas Outlet** in Tías.

Bacon wrapped around chipolata sausages can be purchased in Ropers, they also have bacon wrapped around dates (datiles) which are delicious as an alternative. Of course you can buy bacon and sausages and make your own – bags of English style sausages can be found in the freezer at Eurospar together with Danish bacon, the streaky bacon is on the cold meat section or off the deli counter.

Gravy powder / granules are British supermarket, Gangas items.

Brussel sprouts and parsnips can occasionally be found fresh if you buy them as soon as they arrive before Christmas otherwise its the freezer section of Ropers or Gangas.

Mince pies, Christmas cake and pudding are British supermarket items including the ingredients to bake your own so add that them your list for Gangas.

Bags of frozen sausage rolls can be bought from Gangas.

If I've missed something off your Christmas shopping list please comment below and I'll tell you where you can find it!

Drink

I like a bit of fizz for Christmas, whether its Bucks Fizz with breakfast or a glass before the meal. Spanish cava does not need to be expensive, I love the El Grifo Malvasia Brut but at €11.50 per bottle it has to be a very special occasion. Look out for Siglo XXI in Eurospar, this week it was on offer at an incredible €1.95 per bottle, although I haven't paid more than €3 per bottle for this and it's in stock all year round.

There's loads of choice for beers from Germany and the UK as well as the local brews of Tropical and Dorada. If you're on a budget this Christmas look out for the cases of Wuld available for just under €9.

You will have tasted the Canary Islands Ron Miel (honey rum) normally given as a chupito at the end of a meal in a Lanzarote restaurant, this is the perfect drink to enjoy with your coffee, either serve in a shot glass or over ice.

Toys

The larger toy shops are situated in Playa Honda close to the airport. Mega Centro was where we used to shop when the kids were younger, go downstairs and to the right to find the toy section. The **Deiland** shopping centre is also good place to visit, they have Imaginarium which is similar to the Early Learning Centre on the ground floor and Juguetería Fantasy in the basement for toys, upstairs there is Imagen y Sonido for electrical gifts including games and consoles. For cheaper items and stocking fillers Lanzarote now has a plethora of Euro / Baratísimo shops run by Chinese families.

Wrapping Paper & Cards

English style cards are available from Gangas, gift wrap is almost everywhere and most of the shops will ask if you would like them to wrap the item (¿está esto para un regalo?) at Christmas.

Trees, Decorations & Fireworks

Real Christmas trees are available from Flower Power, fake trees together with lights and decorations can be found in the Euro shops, Mega Centro, Gangas etc. **Fireworks** (Fuego Artificiales / Pirotecnia) can be bought from specialist shops, please click the link for more details.

Gluten free shopping

Lots of concerned holidaymakers contact us prior to their visit to find out where they can buy special dietary foods in Lanzarote.

We'd like to build a list of shops stocking specialist products in Lanzarote to help people suffering with food allergies such as lactose intolerance, dairy or wheat sensitivity and coeliac disease.

We would love your input as to what you've found where, please let us know in comments below and we'll keep this page updated. Between us we can help new visitors to the island know where to source the products they need, when they arrive on the island.

Specialist Shops

Ecotienda Habitat in C.C. Arrecife

Herbarium situated between Pueblo Marinero and C.C. Las Maretas, Avenida Islas Canarias in Costa Teguise

Herbolario Jalea Real in C.C. Mercadillo on Calle Real in Arrecife

Herbolario Ecocentro in C.C. Deiland in Playa Honda

Herbolario El Alquimista on Calle Góngora in Arrecife

Hespérides in Casa Leon, Leon y Castillo in Teguise

Kamila Grosmut on Calle Antonio María Manrique in Teguise

Tienda Verde on Calle Libertad in Tías

Supermarkets

Eurospar stock both Schär and Gullón products as well as soya milk and yoghurts.

Products

Rice milk - Herbolario El Alquimista

Rice milk, soya milk, almond milk & oat milk - Herbarium

Manufacturers

Schär state they are the experts in gluten free food. We have various shops in Lanzarote who stock their range of products such as gluten free bread, pasta, snacks, biscuits, cereals and flour.

Gullón are a biscuit company, founded in 1892 and one of the top three in Spain. They have a health and fibre range of biscuits covering gluten, salt and sugar free varieties which are stocked in the local supermarkets.

Spanish Translation

Sin – without

Trigo – wheat

Gluten – gluten

Sucre – sugar

Sal – salt

Leche – milk

Soja – soya

Celiac – celíaca

Coeliac – celíaco

Sin productos lácteos por favour – no dairy products please

Telephones and internet

Landline and ADSL

I'm sorry to say that customer service isn't Telefonica's strong point, oh they're always polite and ask if you want to complain but actually getting the job done can be difficult. For those of you who don't know who Telefonica is, they are our local telephone and internet service provider, over the recent years there have been some competitors moving into Lanzarote, but they don't yet cover the whole island or you still need a Telefonica landline before you can connect to them.

If you would like a landline telephone or landline including ADSL you need to have your Spanish bank account 20 digit number, your Lanzarote address, your **NIE/F** or passport number, and your existing contact telephone number handy.

Here are the current offers shown on the **Telefonica website**, you have a choice of:

Option 1. Telephone and 6mb internet connection, installation free, telephone €13.97 per month, internet including free WIFI router 29.90 per month for the first year and then increasing to €40.90 per month.

Option 2. Telephone and 6mb internet connection, installation €39.95, telephone €13.97 per month, internet including router and television decoder €32.90 per month for the first year and then increasing to 43.90 per month.

Option 3. Telephone and 10mb internet connection (limited areas), installation free, telephone €13.97 per month, internet including WIFI router €33.90 per month for the first year and then increasing to €44.90 per month.

Option 4. Telephone and 10mb internet connection, installation €39.95, telephone €13.97 per month, internet including router and television decoder €36.90 per month for the first year and then increasing to €47.90 per month.

Television is the Imagenio service, there are three options, but the pricing differences are not made clear on the website……

Imagenio Conexión – click to see the channels, basic but ok if you're not really into watching TV.

Imagenio Basico – click to see the available channels, more than 30 of them.

Imagenio Familiar – click to see channels, about 70 channels, we watch the Fox and AXN channels on Vía y Canal satellite and you can change the language on them, they are mostly American series such as House, ER, Lost, Desperate Housewives, CSI, Dexter, Boston Legal etc. The Option 2 offer is €41.90 a month with this television package.

You can order Telefonica services online but their website is only in Spanish, they do have some online offers only so it might be worth a browse through before you make a call.

Once you've established which package is the right one for you, and you have your paperwork ready, call 1004 from a **Movistar mobile** or any Telefonica call box, you will get a Spanish automated answering service but in the gap or when you hear 'dime' say "English" and you should be transferred to an English speaking operator.

They will talk you through the offers, take your details, if you're ordering ADSL they may ask if you have a computer or laptop and which operating system you're using to determine which router to allocate, so make sure you know before you call.

On the website there is a telephone number for foreigners which it lists as (French, German & English), 917 073 921 – give it a go, its a new one on me!

Once you've placed the order you need to wait for the engineer to call, they quote 7-28 days but its normally within a week, they will ring in Spanish, probably with little or no English and want to come within 10 minutes notice! If the property has had a phone line before, its normally a connection at the exchange and then a quick test at your end to check its working. If the property has not had a line before you may have one of the following problems:

* there aren't any spare lines available

* if its a new build, then there may not be a Telefonica junction box on the complex or not laid in the road as yet

* there is a phone line but either the ADSL or Imagenio service isn't available in your area yet

If you have had a new internet connection installed, your router is sent by courier and only activated on receipt, this rarely coincides with the engineers visit, the best scenario is that you have received the router in advance so the engineer can connect this up, otherwise you will need to activate it and put in your password etc later. Any problems you will be referred to the Tecnico department and help is in Spanish only.

I wish you the very best of luck, Telefonica is a swear word in Lanzarote! Feel free to post your Telefonica experience below, I've got one or two of my own I might add!

Movistar Mobiles

Phones and accessories are available from the Informatica stationery shops situated in the Biosfera Plaza -Puerto del Carmen, Deiland Centre - Playa Honda and Arrecife.

Pay as you go mobiles start from around €50 with €20 credit on the sim card.

Messages

Activate your answer phone by calling 123 or online in Canal Cliente.

The first time you call your voice messages you will need to set up your pin code, the default is 1234. This pin code allows you to listen to your messages from another phone and from abroad.

To set up your personal greeting on the voicemail call 126 and follow the instructions.

The phone will text / call you to inform you that you have received a voice message.

Listen to your voice messages press and hold 1 or dial 123.

To listen to your messages from another mobile or landline call 609123123, you will need your pin code set up when the voice mailbox was set up.

The menu options when you call the voice mailbox are:

Press 0 for help
Press 4 to repeat the message
Press 5 to hear the telephone number that called
Press 7 to delete the message
Press 8 to call the person back
Press 9 to save the message
Press # to skip to the next message

Diverts

To set up diverts if the phone is not answered, choose from:

Activate message if phone is switched off or out of cover call 501.
Activate message if the phone is not answered call 502.
Activate message if the phone is engaged call 503.
Activate message for all calls you receive not answered 504.

To de-activate your voicemail call 537 and press one of the following options:

Press 1 to de-activate when engaged
Press 2 to de-activate when you don't respond
Press 3 to de-activate when off or out of cover
Press 4 to de-activate for all.

Credit

Check your pay as you go credit balance *133# press send and the balance will be sent by text.

You can top up your credit by using one of the machines in the Informatica shops listed above, via your bank online from your account or online on the Movistar website.

Top up online go to **www.movistar.es**
Select móvil, recarga y saldo from the menu options
Enter your mobile number (número de móvil)
Select how much you want to top up from €5 (importe a recargar)
Enter your credit card details (Visa / Mastercard)
Press aceptar
You can top up from 5-30 euros to a maximum of 30 euros per month.

Language

Change the language on your mobile screen, look for idiomas in your menu options and select Ingles!

Online

You can register online go to **www.movistar.es**
Select particulares, then mi movistar then regístrate, you need your passport or residencia to register then you can:

Check your points
Invoices
Call details
Recharge your mobile
Consult your balance

Customer Service

Dial 4554 from your mobile or 638 900 900 from another network or landline for customer service available from

9am to 10pm 7 days a week. To speak in English dial 4431 and select option 1.

Vodafone Mobiles

Phones and accessories are available from the shop situated on Calle José Antonio where it becomes three lanes exiting Arrecife, on the right hand side.

Voice Messages

Listen to your voice messages dial 177 any new messages will be played. If you have old messages you want to listen to press 1. After each message you will be given the following options in Spanish, press 1 to return the call, press 3 to delete any messages, 5 to listen to the telephone number and 6 for the time the message was left.

To listen to your messages from another mobile or landline call 607177177 enter your mobile telephone number then # and your password then #.

To cancel the message service #147#ENV if you add ##002# this cancels all personal options.

For customer service call 132 from your mobile. They will set up your voice message service and change your voice message phone menu into English for you.

Credit

Check your credit by typing *111# send or calling 123.

You can top up your credit by using one of the machines in the Vodafone shop, via your bank online from your account or online on the Vodafone website.

To top up online click **Vodafone** and select particulares and then recarga tu tarjeta
Enter the mobile phone number (Introduce el número de teléfono que quieres recargar)
Click the tarjeta bancaria credito / debito
Minimum top up is 5 euros and maximum 90.

Diverts

To divert your phone to answer phone if you are out of coverage or switched off:

Switched off / Out of Cover / Occupied - 15 seconds then send *147#ENV
Switched off / Out of Cover / Occupied - 30 seconds then send *147*30#ENV
Switched off / Out of Cover - 15 seconds then send *147*1#ENV
Unconditional then send *147*2#ENV

Online

You can also control your mobile phone on the internet, go to **Vodafone** then select particulares and Mi Vodafone to register your phone and then you can:

Consult your points
Manage your invoice
Change your tariff
Details of your calls
Recharge your phone online
Activate your answering machine

Customer Service

Dial 123 from your mobile, they can set up international roaming, activate your message service and much more.

Business and jobs

Jobs in Lanzarote

This time of year, we get many requests about jobs on the island – I guess people are looking to get away from the gloom of northern Europe and to enjoy some of our sunshine.

I thought it would be a good time to talk about getting a job here.

The Market

We don't have a sophisticated employment market here, with agencies and large classified sections in newspapers. Most jobs pass around the island via word of mouth – we publish all those we hear about, but there are probably many we don't. What that means is that, unless you're looking for a job with a big travel company, who advertises abroad, it's pretty much impossible to get a job here, unless you are actually on the island.

My advice to anyone looking to move and work here is to arrive with enough money to live on for a few months. Print off a load of CV's, including a colour headshot of yourself and get a local mobile phone number, and hit the streets, telling everyone you are looking for work. Sooner or later, the right person will hear of the right opening, and you'll get a call.

We don't have big industry, or big administration centres here, so the chances of getting factory or office work are pretty much zero.

The market revolves around tourism, and all the ancillary services that feed that market.

Language

If you only speak English, you are very much limiting yourself to businesses that work exclusively in the English speaking market. it doesn't mean you won't find work, but if you speak Spanish, you'll have more than ten times the options available to you. German is also useful, as are most European languages.

Contracts

Under Spanish law businesses that take on employees must provide them with a work contract. This is expensive for them, and some companies will try to offer jobs without a contract. If you are tempted to start a job on that basis, then be aware that you won't legally be "in the system" for healthcare or any redundancy or other benefits, and you won't be entitled to any of the usual protections for employees.

Pay

Pay is lower here than in most northern European countries, but the upside is the cost of living is also lower! Pay for bar work can be under €10 an hour, and for a full time administrative job less than €1500 a month.

Multiple Jobs

There are plenty of part time jobs on the island, so many people combine two or even three jobs to create one full time job. That also gives you the security of some income even if one them finishes.

Work for yourself or start a business

This is the other option. It's quite easy to become self employed here – you'll have to register for income tax and pay a monthly social security charge of around €250. Self employed is called Autónomo. You can also set your own business up, and in that case we'd advise you to talk to a Asesoría about applying for the various licences.

Tips for getting a job in Lanzarote

At this time of year we are always contacted by lots of people from Northern Europe asking about moving to the island and working here. It makes sense, of course. Faced with the prospect of it getting dark in mid afternoon, and cold weather, with rain and snow on the horizon, we understand the attraction of coming to join us all working in the sunshine here.

So here are some quick tips for anyone thinking about coming to work over here, for the winter or for the long term.

1/ You need to be here!

It's almost impossible to get a job in Lanzarote without actually being on the island to go for an interview! Realistically, very few businesses are going to take an employee on via email or on the strength of a phone interview. My advice, if you are serious, is to come here armed with enough money to live on for a few months, and then to look for work.

2/ Be open-minded

The island doesn't really have any industry, and most jobs are related to the tourist industry. If your experience is in factory work, for example, there's almost none of that here, so you'll have to keep an open mind about what you do want to do.

3/ Consider multiple jobs

There are a lot of part time jobs here, so one option to make up a full time salary, is to take two or more jobs on initially.

4/ Prepare a one page CV

Keep it to a summary as a one pager, and put a headshot image onto it. Keep your full CV available for anyone who wants to know more.

5/ Be proactive!

There aren't Job Centres here and job vacancies are often not even advertised, so the best way to secure work is to get out and about and tell as many people as possible you are looking for work. Invest in a local mobile telephone, some contact cards and print off copies of your one page CV and leave them wherever you can when you are out and about. Plenty of news travels here via word of mouth, so the more people who know who you are and what you are doing, the better.

Also, identify companies who may be interested in you and contact them to let them know you are here – you might just time it perfectly, and even if you don't, they might be recruiting again in the near future.

6/ Use social media well

Many businesses and residents use social media here, so make sure you have a profile on Facebook and Twitter, and be active in the various Lanzarote groups and pages. Remember that prospective employers may check you out on social media, so keep that in mind!

7/ Stay positive!

It can be tough looking for work in a foreign country, but take heart from the fact that many people have come to the island over the last decades and plenty of them have created new lives for themselves here.

8/ Learn some Spanish

Some Spanish language (or German!) is a positive benefit, and if you can speak Spanish fluently, you'll massively increase your chances of getting work here.

Finally, Spain has been seriously affected by the recession, although here in Lanzarote, we have fared better than the peninsular. But times are tough for many businesses, jobs aren't growing on trees, and salaries are significantly lower than in many countries. We haven't written that to put you off, but you need to be aware of the facts before you make the big move.

Running a business

Running a business in Lanzarote is pretty straightforward, although you do need to be sure that you have the necessary licenses to do so. An abogado (lawyer) or an asesoría (accountant) can do this for you. If you have business premises you will need to make sure you have a licence for those as well, this is called a Licencia de Apertura.

Your business can be run by you as a self employed person, in which case you will be trading as an individual, as a partnership or as a limited company.

As an individual, you should refer to our article of being **self employed** here in Lanzarote.

A partnership is referred to here as an SCP. You can have as many partners in the business as you like and they are all responsible jointly for the business and should have a share of the profits based on their share of the business. You will need a constitution for the business, which defines the role and scope of the company. The business will be issued a fiscal ID number of a CIF.

A limited company here is called SL, and all of the above applies, but additionally the SL must have an administrador named (effectively the managing director) who takes responsibility for the correct running of the organization. Rules and regulations are quite strong for an SL, but you will enjoy the protection that your liability is limited in the event of the business failing. You must have at least €3000 of capital to set an SL up, and this must remain in the company at all times, either in the form of cash or assets.

Lanzarote is still behind the times in terms of the products and services available to residents and tourists, therefore there are many opportunities for entrepreneurs to start new businesses here. Perhaps start by thinking of the things you have in your home country, which are not yet available her. One example would be a decent take away shop service!

Another option is to consider buying an existing business. There are many for sale on the island, ranging from a window cleaning round at €4000 to a hotel for several Million!

Self employment

Being self employed in Lanzarote, or any part of Spain is not only easy, but also much more common than in other European countries.

The Spanish word for self employment is Autónomo, when you register as autónomo you immediately start paying into the social security system and therefore receive entitlement to the local medical health system. The easiest way to set up your business is to work with an asesoría, they will make sure that the correct forms are completed and any necessary licenses required applied for. In almost call cases you will be required to charge IGIC, which is our equivalent to VAT, and in this case your asesoría will make a quarterly IGIC return on your behalf. The current rate of IGIC in the Lanzarote and the rest of the Canary islands is 7%.

When self employed you can opt to either make quarterly IGIC and income tax declarations or pay a fixed quarterly amount on the modulos system both have their advantages:

Quarterly declarations – the benefit is that you only pay tax on the actual income earned / declared but need to submit your invoices and receipts usually through an accountant.

Modulos system – simple, fixed cost and no book keeping but payable regardless of results.

As a self employed person in Lanzarote, you are free to earn your income from a number of sources, and it's quite common for people to have 3 or 4 "jobs" where they charge for their services by invoice. Be sure all the money you earn goes through your bank account, as this will help with getting finance in the future.

Work Contracts

Work contracts in Spain are sought after and provide strong protection for employees. You employer will pay your social security and is responsible for collecting your income tax before paying your net salary. Income tax rates are a maximum of 18%, but are often significantly lower depending on earnings, but you will be required to complete a tax return every year, and the good news is that you will usually get a rebate! It's recommended that you use the services of an Asesoría (an accountant) who will do your return for you.

Having your social security paid will give you, your spouse and children full health cover and an entitlement (after 2 years) to both the very generous unemployment benefit in case of redundancy, and to a pension. Spain is also a great place to work in terms of holidays, there are 30 days per year plus fiesta days for full time workers. Labour costs in Spain are high, so many employers pay a low basic salary (as costs are based on the amount paid) and top up with cash. This is not legal, but nevertheless it is common practice.

Types of Contract

There are two different types of work contract, indefinite or temporary. A temporary contract can be issued if the role is for training, replacement of an employee for a specific time or for completion of a specific time related job. An indefinite contract can be issued for part or full time roles.

Your contract should include both details of you and your employer, start date, type of contract, profession, number of days holiday entitlement, description of your working hours and specification of any trial period. The contract must be signed by both parties and stamped by Oficina Nacional de Empleo – the Employment Office.

Minimum Working Conditions

The Estatuto de Trabajadores describes the minimum working conditions for jobs in Spain. The standard work week is 40 hours, maximum hours per day is 9 with a rest of 12 hours before your next shift, all workers should have uninterrupted rest of one and a half days per week. There are **14 national holidays** defined in the Calendario Laboral for the region and 30 calendar days. Overtime is restricted to 80 hours per year. All of these can be negotiated under the collective bargaining depending upon the role as long as the employee is compensated.

Deductions

The minimum annual salary is approximately 600 Euros per month, if you are earning over this amount your employer will deduct monthly contributions from your wages. Social security is currently 6.4% of your taxable income and paid to the Tesorería General de la Seguridad Social, your employer will be asked to deduct personal income tax at the level determined by your self assessment annual returns, the general tax free allowance is 5,151 Euros per year.

The work ethic is different to many northern European countries - people in Spain work to live, rather than the other way around!

Company sizes in Lanzarote

Many people considering moving to Lanzarote want to know about the possibilities they have of finding a job where they can continue their chosen career path.

Generally for expats the chance of working in a larger organisations is limited unless you are fluent in at least one foreign language, Spanish is a must with German an advantage, as together with English these are the three main languages spoken on the island.

I've just read a recent study into the size of companies here in Lanzarote which was published this week by the Cabildo's data centre.

Seven companies in Lanzarote have at least 250 staff, 3 of these companies are based in Arrecife, 2 in Yaiza and 1 each in San Bartolomé and Tinajo.

Medium sized companies are considered entities with more than 50 employees but less than 250, there are 85 such companies registered in Lanzarote. They are located in 19 Arrecife, 12 San Bartolomé, 25 Teguise, 16 Tías and 13 Yaiza.

There are 5,531 smaller businesses on the island, these are classed as up to 50 employees but often it can be as low as one or two staff. The companies are shown as located in the following municipalities 2613 Arrecife, 1,197 Tías, 661 Teguise, 474 San Bartolomé, 375 Yaiza, 107 Tinajo and 104 Haría.

The End!

You've reached the end of this guide to relocating to Lanzarote, but your journey is probably just starting! We'd like to wish you the very best of luck and we hope one day to add you to our ever increasing circle of friends based here on the island.

If you need more help or advice, we offer a one hour relocation consultation service, which costs €26.75. Be prepared with a huge list of questions! If there are any we don't know the answers to during the call, we'll find out and email them to you afterwards.

If you'd like to take us up on it, just send an email to Miguel@lanzaroteinformation.com and we'll set it all up for you.

Good luck!